Thinking Golf

Thinking Golf

DAVID FOSTER

PELHAM BOOKS · LONDON

First published in Great Britain by
PELHAM BOOKS LTD
44 Bedford Square
London WC1
1979

ISBN 0 7207 1169 X

Typeset in Great Britain by Granada Graphics and printed
and bound by Billings and Sons, Guildford

Contents

Acknowledgements

In writing this book I have been greatly helped by some golfers I know and some I have never met. I acknowledge my debt to:

The Science of The Golf Swing (Pelham Books) by Dr David Williams – for his convincing explanation that the golf swing is a flail action.

The Search for The Perfect Swing (Heinemann) by Alistair Cochran and John Stobbs, which contains a wealth of scientific data about the game and which should be at every golfer's bedside.

The International Sports Company — with whom we associate such famous names as Dunlop and Slazenger and who freely gave me access to their technical files and provided me with experimental golf clubs.

The Committee of the Berkshire Golf Club, who welcomed my electronic monster DOC into that club of golfing excellence and to the many members of that club who collaborated in the experiments.

Mr Keith MacDonald, the professional at the Berkshire Golf Club, and his two assistants. **Mr Andrew Hall** and **Mr Andrew Reynolds**, for professional golfing advice and for keeping me on the rails when I might have run off the track. I am particularly grateful to **Mr Henry Cotton** both for writing the Foreword and also for the pre-publication article he wrote in *Golf Monthly* a little while back. Mr Cotton has a unique place in golf history being the one who established golf as a highly respected profession, and I well remember that battle he fought virtually single-handed in the 1930s to bring this about. When we enjoy golf on television with famous names jetting-in from all over the world, it is fun to think that forty years later the pioneer is still at it in the commentary box. Nor may younger players using the Dunlop '65' golf ball realise that the '65' is a testimonial to Henry's record-breaking round in a British Open Championship.

White House   David Foster
Sunninghill Road
Windlesham
Surrey
England

Foreword
by Henry Cotton M.B.E.

I had great fun reading this golf book by David Foster; in fact I digested every word, and that says a lot in my case, as I have been in golf as a professional for well over fifty years and have 'seen it all and read most of it too'.

The title of this book, *Thinking Golf*, can be taken in two distinct ways. In the first place in terms of armchair 'thinking about golf' and in the second place as to 'thoughtful golf' on the actual course. For this latter interpretation David Foster has coined the term 'Psycho-Golf'. The book deals with both interpretations.

It is surprising to me to find so many of my own beliefs about the game in this book. I have always felt that I knew what I was talking about despite so many differing ideas being sold to the golfing world at large. I have always thought that there must be others on my side, and David Foster is one.

His work is full of golf science and electronic experimentation to prove the points he makes. Thus he built apparatus to measure all aspects of the impact between club and ball, and to measure muscular strength, human reaction times and club whippiness.

Golf, he rightly claims, is for everyone, and this book is directed to the average golfer. This is the right approach, because champions who give their names to the 'How I do it' books start with ideal physiques for striking a golf ball well. It is here that David Foster introduces his concept of Psycho-Golf with its drill words (useful 'gimmicks' I call them), to help the golfer remember how to set up the shot and to compensate for not being a born golfer.

In my own teaching of golfers I have come across those who like to use reminder words to set up the swing, and this can be a useful method for those who normally sit at their desks all day. David Foster takes this method to its logical conclusion and advocates that the golfer should define his own Golfing Formula of only three single syllable words which the golfer can remember without 'running out of mental stretch'. These ideas are a pleasure to read and think about.

David Foster has experimented with golf clubs and with methods of striking and of obtaining a reliable swing and often gives the results of his experiments on easily understood charts. How right he is when he claims that the secret of successful play is to hit the centre of the back of the ball with the centre of the club face, and this applies to all of us. I have always called this 'finding the ball' but David Foster spells it out as to accuracy requirements in fractions of an inch and circular degrees.

Human beings are not built to perform athletic feats with the body all twisted at the start of their golf stroke action but, as the author states, these distortions have to be understood and circumvented. David Foster does a good job in trying to help everyone understand 'how he or she stands and swings' and why.

To develop the reader's curiosity he describes Four Impact Imperatives and Five Laws of Cussedness. None of us would dispute his Four Impact Imperatives, which are described in most good golf books. But his addition of Five Laws of Cussedness is novel. The first four show how the human being finds it so difficult to emulate a simple swinging mechanical pendulum of the sort which all golf ball makers have and which can land ten balls within a five-yard diameter at a full drive distance.

But his Fifth Law of Cussedness, that the golfer runs

out of mental stretch in trying to remember all he ought to do when taking his stroke is the common experience of professional and amateur alike: 'I forgot to remember'. It is this fact which takes him to the heart of his argument in favour of Psycho-Golf: how to simplify and put that simplification into a few well-chosen words as one shapes up to that small white ball.

So here is wishing the golf student Happy Days both with *Thinking Golf* in general and Psycho-Golf in particular. I am sure everyone will find it fun.

Well done, David Foster!

Henry Cotton

Introduction

This book did not start as a planned enterprise. Some four years ago, in 1975, I found myself retired from business affairs. Being a Typical Golfer of fifty years' standing and having some knowledge of electronics I decided to build an electronic robot (DOC) which would instrument the nature of the golfer's impact with the ball. It was fun. But it seems that when one starts scientifically measuring facts related to fun situations there can be surprises. This certainly happened to me as I found myself in the possession of new factual knowledge about golf and from that time I decided to write a book about my experience.

I imagine that this book is about as unlike the sort of book a professional golfer might write as is conceivable. The professional golfer has acquired his skills over many years of experience and practice so that his skills essentially reside in his muscles. But the Typical Golfer such as myself does not have time for such practice and thus his only resource is to make up by thinking what he lacks in muscle know-how. This book is a challenge on this issue. It is a challenge to the Typical Golfer to show that his power of thought might to some degree compensate for his lack of professional physical skill and that is why the book is called *Thinking Golf*.

If the power of thought is to substitute for lack of golfing practice, then one needs to start with certain facts about the game and also to have a consistent theory or mental model based on those facts. It was this which I found was lacking in searching the available golfing literature. Those who write books about golf are mainly famous professional golfers and perhaps they lack the expertise to convey their muscular know-how in a book. But it was also possible that there was something odd about the game which no one had understood.

On further study of the matter I decided that the latter was true and that there really *was* a mystery about golf and this was because its essential nature had been misjudged. The true essence of golf is that it is a *system problem* and the professional golfer copes with the situation by constant practice so that eventually the system is automatically integrated so that he becomes more like a well-oiled machine. Typical separate parts of the system problem are such vital but distinct factors as grip, stance and swing and although the professional golfer by practice can integrate these into a whole, for the Typical Golfer they remain as distinct and separate parts of his stroke. Thus the only hope for the Typical Golfer who wishes to improve his game is to integrate the separate vital aspects of the golf stroke by *conscious co-ordination*. But it appears that no one knows how to achieve conscious co-ordination of complex physical acts and certainly no one knows how to write a book about it.

Now in ordinary life we are quite used to co-ordinating complex systematic problems ('organising' or 'managing') because there is normally plenty of time to think about the different factors and their optimum co-ordination. But the problem in golf is that the whole stroke as to backswing and downswing only takes about one second and our processes of analytical and synthetic thought are far too slow to intervene in and control such a fast physical phenomenon. Thus the problem of our inadequate golfing knowledge is:

No one knows how to bring the conscious mind to bear in a controlling fashion on fast physical processes whose duration is of the order of one second

This implies that the Typical Golfer has to play the game in a fashion which is virtually *mindless*.

All a golfer could do was either to practice for a great deal of time so that 'control' was automatised but this is ruled out for the Typical Golfer who has other things to do than play golf. Alternatively, the Typical Golfer can opt out of taking the game seriously and just have a bit of fresh air and fun. I think this is the main decision and experience. Nevertheless this is not a satisfactory state of affairs since the human being is a creature whose higher states of satisfaction depend upon a sense of skilful achievement. Thus while such opting out has given rise to an endless spate of fun-books about golf it does not affect the fact that every Typical Golfer hopes that his next stroke will be 'the shot of the match'.

I think my diagnosis that the control problem in the golf stroke is because the human mind cannot intervene in very fast processes will be accepted by most golfers. The human mind, and I emphasise the word 'mind', takes several seconds to focus on an idea. Thus to think about three or so different ideas during the golf stroke is impossible, or so it would seem. But this means that the golfer's most valuable instrument of intelligence, his 'word mind', is almost useless to him. This is not a matter of the golfer being stupid but is due to the psychological fact that our word mind works much slower than our physical skills. We can *do* something far faster than we can consciously *think* about it. Thus the problem of Psycho Golf is a technical problem related to the relative speeds of psychic processes.

It is the solution to this problem which is the central quest in this book and which crystalises in Part 3, on Psycho-Golf. I found the solution in the expression 'word-drill' in that there is a process of psycho-physical co-ordination in which *a single word can control a complex act of behaviour*. The solution had been discovered by the military in the need to control a large number of people ('as one man') both on the field of battle and by training ('drill') on the barracks square. A good example is that of a sergeant-major pronouncing the word 'atten...shun!' A group of soldiers, in almost exact unison, will each carry out *four* precise skilled movements in *less than one second* (actually in about .3 second). I felt sure that this was the clue to any development of a new method of playing golf in which the word mind could be brought to bear in controlling physical acts. Barracks square drill was an example of how *one word* could control a fast physical act. It is this method which I elaborate as Psycho-Golf.

The book is divided into three parts.

In Part 1 I make the case that golf is a systems problem and that a good golf stroke has to meet Four Impact Imperatives while at the same time avoiding or circumventing Five Laws of Cussedness. The Impact Imperatives and the Laws of Cussedness are mainly physical and can be defined exactly. One does not need to explore the emotional aspects of golf to define its inherent mechanical system complexity.

Part 2 of the book is concerned with the laboratory type of experiments I made on how the golfer impacts the ball. In this quest I also discovered curious facts about the golfer himself. Perhaps the most important discovery was the division of golfers into Speed and Power Types, with the latter predominating. The Speed Golfer is one who can swing lighter clubs substantially faster than heavier clubs and thus bears witness to Dr David Williams' claim that we may be playing with far too heavy equipment. But I also found that the majority of golfers are Power Golfers who cannot take advantage of lighter clubs since they cannot swing their bodies as fast as their arms. Such golfers have to slow down consciously to get their best effects. This restricts them to the use of heavier clubs.

Part 3 is on Psycho-Golf itself and expresses the view

that to improve his golf the Typical Golfer *must* find a way to make greater use of his conscious mind to compensate for his lack of routine practice. This involves *a search for simplicity* both as to physical and mental techniques and I hope to show that this can bring the Typical Golfer to the point where his conscious mind is useful to him in programming his golf stroke accurately.

This first involves the construction of a general Mental Model of the game based on the common fundamentals of the Four Impact Imperatives and the Five Laws of Cussedness but also taking into account certain idiosyncrasies of the individual such as his 'Type'. From this general Mental Model a much more brief Skeleton Model must be distilled, which can be represented in only three words – what I call the Golfing Formula – with one word each to represent the essential desirable nature of Grip, Stance and Swing. This brings us into the territory of 'word drill' already referred to.

Psycho-Golf works to the degree to which one understands the fundamental principles involved and has confidence in it. At all times it means that one can immediately refer a bad shot to one's Skeleton Mental Model and be pretty sure of making an immediate, and correct, correction by using one's grey matter in the right fashion.

I would point out to the reader that in this book there is no trace of Golf Mythology or Golf Mystique for I fancy that those two concepts belong to that aspect of a golfer which is 'brute force and bloody ignorance'. Nor am I advocating an artistic approach to golf because I do not think that knocking a little white ball into a hole is an artistic enterprise. But, if this book had a sub-title I would adapt the title of a book by Bernard Shaw and hope that it might be 'An Intelligent Man's Guide to Golf'.

To all my readers I wish 'Good Psycho-Golfing'.

David Foster

PART ONE

Preliminary Thoughts

1

The Unique Fascinating Frustration of Golf

The game of golf is one of the most popular of all sports and its millions of adherents form a very large and active international sporting community. The reason for this popularity is simple, in that golf is a very healthy occupation calling for three hours in the open air under pleasant environmental conditions and it is a sport which can be played from the age of ten years to ninety years. Golf does not call for strength but it calls for an odd sort of skill and I think that it is this particular aspect which is the centre of its fascinating attraction.

But golf is also a very frustrating game. When we are on the first tee we hope to go round in better than our handicap and in nine cases out of ten we do much worse and hence our frustration. No-one ever knows in advance whether he will play well or badly and yet everyone seeks the Philosopher's Stone or 'secret of golf' which will end the fascinating frustration.

Yesterday at my own club, the Berkshire, I watched a golfer drive off the tee and slice the ball 45 degrees to the right onto the next fairway. In disgust he put down a second ball and did exactly the same thing. Two worse successive shots one could hardly imagine and yet in his previous round that same golfer had done a hole-in-one at the 230 yard sixteenth on our Red Course which must be one of the most difficult of all holes-in-one. This is 'super-frustration' and 'super-fascination'.

The fascination in golf is that all this frustration is

accurately measured by the total score, the total number of strokes one takes to get round, and thus the frustration is quantified in a fashion with which no other game can compare. In almost all other walks of life, whether at work or play, there is *no exact measurement of performance* to compare with the golfer on the golf course. This is why the game particularly fascinates the Americans who are addicted to numbers and counting whether in dollars or golf scores. We have all heard of the 'I.Q.' (Intelligence Quotient) in which the mentality of people can (supposedly) be represented on a numerical scale like degrees on a thermometer and most of us are glad quietly to opt out of such personal measurement. But on the golf course one cannot opt out and if one gets round in 96 strokes against a par of 72 it suggests that one has had 24 thoroughly bad shots (96 − 72) and there is no evading the numerical evidence which is marked on one's golf card and witnessed and signed for. Indeed, if there is a path of measured humility in life it is related to the factual score which a golfer has to declare at the end of his round. There is even a case to be made that 'only golfers go to Heaven' since only golfers have their performance measured and thus achieve a remorseless fate.

Thus there is something very special about the game of golf and I think it relates to what I have stated above, which I will now define more accurately:

> *Golf is the only performing experience in the life of the average man in which he is accurately measured*

What the 'Measurement' states – handicaps

I recently studied the male golf handicaps at my own club, The Berkshire, and the analysis showed (per 100 members):

Handicap group	Number of golfers
Scratch – 4	2
5 – 9	20
10 – 14	33
15 – 19	32
20 – 24	13
	——
	100

A little calculation shows that the average handicap is just a little over 13.

'Proper Par' for the Typical Golfer

This book is about, and for, the Typical Golfer with this average handicap of about 13. I have stated that the handicap of the Typical Golfer is 13, but does this mean that he has played thirteen bad shots in each round? I think not, because in setting the Par for a golf course, the system is one of standard distances and these are based on the length-hitting of the professional golfer and should not apply to the Typical Golfer. They are based roughly on the assumption of the following striking distances and on the right I show the good striking distances of the Typical Golfer *playing well*:

Stroke	Professional golfer	Typical amateur golfer
Drive	250 yards	200 yards
Fairway long hit	210 yards	180 yards

Now allowing for two putts a hole, this means that Par-4s can be up to about 460 yards in length and such lengths are virtually *impossible* for the Typical Golfer playing at his best: indeed he will be lucky to reach a 400 yard Par-4 green in two shots. Now at my own Berkshire club we have two courses (the well-known Blue and Red) and allowing for Proper Par for the Typical Golfer then one has to add about four strokes to each course. Thus the Typical Golfer with a handicap of 13 is really playing to nine in terms of *true dropped strokes*. His handicap of 13 is thus made up of two factors:

Bad play. 9 dropped strokes.
Proper Par discrepancy. 4 'impossible' strokes.

I only know one golf club which makes proper allowance for this fact that the course Par is set by the professional golfer and this is Sunningdale where the score card has a column for Par and a column they call Bogey which is what I have been calling Proper Par for the Typical Golfer playing well.

I am not complaining about the setting of Par related to the professional golfer since it is all relative but it becomes very important to make the above correction in considering the vast majority who are Typical Golfers and whose 'perfect round' could never beat 4 over Par at 2 putts per green. I come thus to a conclusion which I shall use later:

The Typical Golfer has a handicap of 13 but only drops about nine true shots when playing to his handicap

'Dropping Shots'

There are only two ways in which we can truly drop golf shots:

1   By failing to reach the green in Proper-Par figures.
2   By taking more than two putts on the green.

In this book I shall only be concerned with the first of the above because many Typical Golfers do average two putts per green and thus their main problem is:

How to reach the green in Proper Par figures

'Dropped shots' are mainly a matter of adding an extra

shot or two between tee and green. At this stage one may wonder how a professional can sometimes go round a Par-72 course in the middle 60s and the answer from my own observations is that he picks up the extra shots partly by reaching the shorter Par-5 hole greens in two shots so that they become Par-4s whilst he can be very accurate in his approaches to the shorter Par-4 holes and can often get down in a single putt.

But such is not for our Typical Golfer whose main problem is how to avoid dropping (say) nine shots between tee and green off his Proper Par handicap.

2
Golf and Systems Theory

I am a professional engineer and we engineers make the following distinctions:

A Machine is a set of components which are *geared* together to operate as a whole without the need for conscious co-ordination between the parts of the machine. Thus the following are machines:

A watch
A motor-car
A lathe
A dish-washer

The co-ordination between the parts of a machine is done by means of gears or levers or linkages of a mechanical or electrical nature so that it automatically operates as a whole.

A System is a set of machines or activities which have to be consciously co-ordinated together to operate effectively and in default of such co-ordination the system will fail. Thus the following are systems:

A factory
An airline
A school
A HUMAN BEING

Now our Typical Golfer hopes to play golf like 'a well-oiled machine' but this is impossible since human activities are *system activities*.

6

Why the human being is a system

A system requires conscious co-ordination to operate effectively. But consider some of the aspects of a human being which are relevant to playing the game of golf:

1 The golfer has within him an *emotional* machine
2 The golfer has within him a *thinking* machine
3 The golfer has within him a *balancing* machine
4 The golfer has within him a *power* machine
5 The golfer has within him a *bio-chemical* or health machine

I name five sorts of machine which go to make up the golfer as a system and I could name more. But note how none of the above five machines has any automatic co-ordination with the others. Indeed, some can easily and obviously be in conflict. Thus:

a) The golfer's *emotional* machine, worrying about his just-played-bad-shot, can interfere with his *thinking* machine about the present shot.

b) The golfer's *power* machine can be at loggerheads with his *balancing* machine so that he is off-balance.

c) The golfer's *bio-chemical* or health machine can be in disarray due to a hangover from the previous evening so that the adrenalin won't flow.

At this stage I only make the point that:

The Typical Golfer is a system of separate factors which require conscious co-ordination for good golf

Systems Reliability mathematics

As soon as one realises that golf is a system problem then one can turn to the highly developed Systems-Science for further illumination and this happens to be one of my own professional specialities.
I define:

*The game of golf is a system activity and calls
for conscious co-ordination under the laws of
System-Science*

System-Science has two main postulates:

1   The success of a system is related to the individual
    performance and *reliability* of its *vital* component
    parts. A vital component is defined as one whose
    failure would fail the total system.

2   System Reliability can be measured by the fol-
    lowing formula:
    System Reliability = $R_1 \times R_2 \times R_3 \times R_4 \ldots$ etc.
    where R_1, R_2 etc. are the known Reliabilities (with
    unity '1' or 100%, as a maximum) of the individual
    vital components.

First Example Let us imagine that I have a business
proposition which involves myself (as Mr A) making a
certain number of telephone calls to a collaborator, Mr
B.

   Now assuming that I ought to make ten telephone
calls to Mr B but I only remember to do so on eight out
of the ten occasions, then my reliability is 8/10 or 80 per
cent. But when I do make a telephone call to Mr B he
only remembers to ring me back again with appropriate
answers on seven out of ten occasions so that his
reliability is 70 per cent.

   The total reliability of such a system involving myself
(Mr A) with my collaborator Mr B is thus:

Systems reliability = 80% × 70% = 56%.

Not too good!

Second Example Mrs A (such as my wife) is an excellent
housekeeper but has to rely on various mechanical aids
which sometimes let her down (in terms of effective days
per 100 days) as follows and expressed as reliability
percentages:

Dishwasher	97%
Ironer	96%
Vacuum Cleaner	98%
Refrigerator	93%
Boiler	94%
Clothes washer	92%

Assuming that she makes equal use of these then what is her maximum efficiency as a 'perfect' housewife?
It is:

$$97\% \times 96\% \times 98\% \times 93\% \times 94\% \times 92\% = 73\%$$

Thus no matter how efficient my wife is as a housekeeper, she cannot perform at better than 73 per cent as limited by the total system reliability of the gadgets on which she depends. And note that each of them is individually above 90 per cent reliable.

Golf as a (possibly) Six Component Reliability System

To continue this line of argument we return to our Typical Golfer who is trying to avoid dropping those (say) nine shots off his Proper Par handicap. Now I am going to suggest that a golfer is a system having six distinct and separate components, the failure of any one of which will cause him to 'drop a shot'. In principle, it does not matter which vital components or how many one defines, but my own judgment is that they may be as follows:

Two psychological components

1　*Emotional poise* If one plays golf in a state of inner emotional 'commotion' such as worrying about previous bad play, hating one's opponent, thinking about the horrors of inflation, then one is apt to 'drop a shot'. This is particularly emphasised in competitions as 'nerves'.

Thus emotional poise or self-possession is a positive requirement which is eroded by the 'commotions' I have briefly touched upon.

2   *Good thinking and judgment*

Is it wise to take a 2-Wood out of heather?

Is it wise to 'play for a slice' when one can normally hardly play a straight shot?

Is it wise to force a 7-Iron when an easy 5-Iron could get one on the green?

The positive requirement is good thinking and good judgment and playing the percentages on the prudent side. Anything else, and one has 'dropped a shot', perhaps two.

Four mechanical requirements

3   *The correct grip* One needs to take such a grip that the probability is that on the downswing and into impact one hits the ball fair and square. A bad grip, and one has 'dropped a shot'.

4   *The correct address* This is the correct lining up of the club to the ball so that one is at the right distance from the ball to make a 'fair and square' impact on the downswing and hit the ball with the club at the centre of percussion. If one hits the ball with the club away from the centre of percussion one has 'dropped a shot'.

5   *The correct stance* This is the correct final posture and hitting attitude and involves a certain balancing and tilting and keeping the right shoulder back. If one gets this wrong, one 'drops a shot'.

6   *The correct swing* The swing has to be 'in one piece'

without overswinging and one must go back on the correct plane. If one gets it wrong, then one has 'dropped a shot'.

I invite my reader to examine any of the above six vital aspects of playing a golf shot and to consider whether it is not true that even if one has five aspects right, the defective sixth vital factor will not cause one to 'drop a shot'.

The staggering reliability mathematics of six-factor systems

Earlier, I gave a simple example of the reliability of my wife as a 'domestic system' in which six vital factors all over 90 per cent efficient gave an overall systems reliability of only 73 per cent. But now we are considering our Typical Golfer as a six-factor system and the results of the mathematics are staggering.

In the first place let us consider that our Typical Golfer has all his six vital components or factors (R_1, R_2, R_3 etc.) at an equal state of reliability. In that case his overall System Reliability will be R^6.

The following table holds:

Vital Component Reliability	System (R^6) Reliability	Handicap or Dropped Shots
100%	100%	0
99%	94%	4
98%	88%	9 *
97%	83%	12
96%	79%	15
95%	73%	19
94%	69%	22
93%	65%	25
92%	61%	28
91%	57%	31
90%	53%	34

* Typical Golfer

In this table we also show the consequent golf handicap (relative to Proper Par) according to the formula for a 72 Par course as Handicap = .72(100 – System Reliability). This is an exact formula since we define vital factor reliability as directly related to the probability of 'dropping a shot'.

Now we note an extraordinary thing in our Typical Golfer who has a nominal average handicap of 13 and is permitted to drop (say) nine shots against his Proper Par:

> *The Typical Golfer is 98 per cent efficient as to average vital factors in his game but this makes his system reliability only 88 per cent*

The conclusions from golf systems theory

The figures I have just calculated should cause all golfers to do some thinking. What I am stating is:

1   Golf is a *system* problem in which (say) six relatively independent factors have each to be correct to obtain a good golf shot.
2   Assuming this, the Typical Golfer dropping nine shots from his Proper Par will require to have his six factors each at 98 per cent efficiency to give him a system efficiency of 88 per cent which corresponds to dropping those nine shots.

Now the idea of doing things at 98 per cent efficiency is almost unheard of in normal life activities and this is why one can play golf for fifty years and never 'break 80'. Golf is an extremely difficult game for the simple reason that one needs to have a lot of factors correct to secure a good stroke and any one factor which is 'below par' will ensure we score above Par.

3

The Golfing Machine
and the Four Impact
Imperatives

There is nothing more annoying than to realise that one can build an artificial golfing machine which will perform scratch golf with no problems. All the golf-ball manufacturers have such machines, golfing robots, (see Fig. 3.1) and they are constructed on the most elementary principles. Such a machine swings a club at the ball but does so in exact conformity with Four Golfing Impact Imperatives:

1   The club face at impact is exactly *square* to the ball.
2   The club face at impact strikes the ball *centrally*, at the 'centre of percussion' or sweet spot of the club face.
3   At the brief period of impact the club is travelling in the exact *direction* of the intended line of flight.
4   At the moment of impact the club has such a *speed* that it is known just how much kinetic energy it will impart to the ball.

Note that all Four Impact Imperatives relate only to the moment of impact and such a golfing robot does not concern itself with such human golfing worries as 'flexible knees', 'get the left hip out of the way', 'keep your eye on the ball', 'don't sway' and the rest of the self-torturing reminders. The reason for this cavalier disregard by a golfing robot is simple in that it does not have knees or hips, it does not have eyes to keep on the ball and it is incapable of swaying.

It is a machine and *not* a multiple-component system requiring conscious co-ordination. The golfing robot is a simple machine in which nothing goes wrong.

Thus the problem of the human golfer is how can he emulate a machine with regard to those four simple Impact Imperatives. All come within the province of Newton's Laws of Motion.

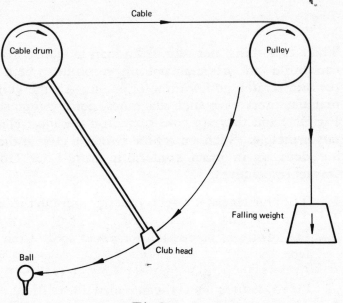

Fig 3.1

Newton's Laws of Motion

It is a strange fact that human golfers drive themselves into desperation to emulate what a simple golfing machine can do with no problems. Now such golfing machines are based on Newton's Laws of Motion and it may be profitable to consider just what these are.

These Laws are three in number and their essence is:

> *First Law* A body in motion will move uniformly in a straight line unless acted upon by some force.

Second Law Change in the motion of a body is proportional to an applied force and the duration of that force and is in the same direction as that force.

Third Law To every forceful action there is an equal and opposite reaction.

The First Impact Imperative – Square Face

It is a *fact* that a golf ball will depart at right angles to the club face. If the club face is ten degrees 'open' then the ball will depart at ten degrees to the right. This is best proved in putting, in that the ball will always depart at right angles to the putter club face at impact. This is the direct result of Newton's Second Law of Motion that the change in motion of a body is in the *same direction* as the applied force.

Very few golfers really understand this. A good test is to hold a putter ten degrees open but strike the ball in an intended correct direction and it will be observed that the ball goes ten degrees to the right.

The initial flight of a golf ball is at right angles to the club face

Thus if one wishes to hit a ball in a specific direction, then the club face must be square to that direction.

The Second Impact Imperative – Central Percussion

We all know that sometimes a ball flies straight and true and we have a sense of hitting it on 'the sweet spot'. But just what is that 'sweet spot'? With properly designed golf clubs it is the centre of the club face (but with bad clubs it is not) and what happens is that the centre of gravity of the club is in line with the ball. Technically speaking this is known as 'the centre of percussion' and this expression means that the 'centre of kinetic energy' is also in line with the ball at impact. If the strike is away from this position then the force has to be transmitted to the ball through bending movements which both twist the club and cause it to generate vibrations. If one hits the ball and the club 'stings' then this is the simplest proof that the ball was struck away from the centre of percussion.

Every part of a golf club has a certain momentum and energy. The 'centre of percussion' is where these are balanced either side of the impact so that there is no net momentum or kinetic energy which is 'off-line'. The size of the 'sweet spot' is quite small and is included within a circle of about ¾-inch diameter described round the centre of the club face.

The Third Impact Imperative – Straightness of Impact

Even if the ball is struck centrally and with a square face, it may still veer off line in a curving arc as to hook or slice. This is due to imparting spin to the ball by cutting across it as to out-to-in (slicing) or in-to-out (hooking). If a golf ball (looking down upon it) has clockwise spin due to hitting from out-to-in then its air resistance is greater in the spin direction and it will veer off oppositely to the right. Conversely for the in-to-out anti-clockwise spin of the hook.

Thus the Third Impact Imperative is to strike the ball with the club moving in the direction of intended line of flight so that no spin is imparted to the ball.

Of all golfing faults, this wrong spin is the most prevalent and is the main reason why golfers finish up off the fairway.

The Fourth Impact Imperative – Club Speed

A golf ball can only travel a distance corresponding to its initial kinetic energy and this in turn depends on the kinetic energy of the club at impact. Since kinetic energy is proportional to the square of speed and since resistance to motion of the ball (aerodynamically) is also proportional to square of speed then the 'squares' cancel out and one can approximate that ball distance will be proportional to club speed at impact.

It is a *fact* that professional golfers swing about 30 per cent faster than the Typical Golfer and thus obtain 30 per cent more distance, say 260 yards with the 1-Wood compared with 200 yards.

Golf course Par figures are measured in terms of length, and a typical length is 6000 yards for a 72-Par. Deducting 36 strokes for putts, this means that the average stroke distance is just on 170 yards. But since the hole distances are not uniformly based on multiples of this distance it is a fair guess, which checks with the facts at my own club, that there will be about nine holes which require a drive of at least 200 yards if one hopes to gain the green in Par figures.

Now 200 yards, and I don't mean sloppy paces, is quite a drive, especially in poor weather and this puts a premium on the ability to generate adequate fast club speed. Every golfer knows that the drive is the most important shot in golf because its consequences must affect all other shots. If the drive goes wrong then one is faced with trying to play 'recovery' shots but these are more difficult than normal shots and thus the dice become loaded against you.

Thus club head speed at impact ranks equal with the other factors already described to qualify as the last of the Four Impact Imperatives.

The irrelevance of golfing methods

The Four Impact Imperatives are the only common ground between a human golfer and a golfing machine. Since a Typical Golfer cannot play nearly as well as a golfing machine, it means that the human being himself is introducing into his golf shots adverse actions. Note that it does not matter what style or idiosyncrasies a golfer may have providing that he establishes the Four Impact Imperatives. This suggests that ideas about 'standard styles' are both irrelevant and confusing. The correct analysis of golf would commence with finding out, for a given golfer, just how he fails to actualise those Four Impact Imperatives.

But next let us consider generally just why it is that a human golfer finds it so difficult to imitate a simple and effective golfing machine.

4

The Requirements
for Accuracy

Let us take stock of the situation we have reached:

1   To hit a good straight golf shot the only basic requirement is to meet those Four Impact Imperatives as to:
   a)   Square face.
   b)   Central ball impact on the club face.
   c)   The club must be travelling in the required direction of flight when it meets the ball.
   d)   Adequate club speed as appropriate.

2   A simple golfing mchine can be made to incorporate the above four features with ease. It would be little more than a powered pendulum.

3   The problem of human golf must be related to the fashion in which the human being departs from being such a simple machine.

Next we consider the accuracy requirements which even a golfing machine must fulfil in meeting those Four Impact Imperatives.

The practical limits to Ideal Accuracy

Golf differs from other ball games in that it is played on a variable terrain. Other ball games such as polo, billiards, tennis and so forth are played under very

19

standard environmental conditions as to the table, pitch or court. But the golfer plays on ground which is always uneven to some degree and he is affected by ground conditions such as softness or hardness and by atmospheric conditions such as rain and wind.

These conditions introduce three sorts of variables into the game which limit the concept of Ideal Accuracy and this would also largely apply to a golfing machine:

Accidental ground conditions at the end of ball flight

From a distance of, say, 150 yards, one may not know that there is a slight hollow in the ground which could cause the ball to bounce to the left or right by several yards. Nor might one take account of a small pool of water only a few feet across which could cause the ball to pull up sharply.

Limitations to distance judgment

I personally cannot judge any distance over one hundred yards to better than ± ten yards. Now since each different club represents an incremental distance of about ten yards then one does well to judge distance to the 'nearest club'. (Frankly I have given up this unequal struggle and only carry 'every other club' in my bag. I am content to rely on my distance judgment for the longer shots to the nearest ± ten yards.)

So let us assume that distance judgment by our Typical Golfer is to ± the nearest ten yards.

Judgment limitations to taking all conditions into account

Other variable factors, each of which can easily introduce variations of plus or minus ten yards, are:
    Wind
    Fall or rise of terrain

Atmospheric 'heaviness' i.e. moisture content of the air including rain.

Ball temperature

All the above factors give distance variations and, at best, I think that if one hits a ball to the nearest ten yards one is performing adequately and will not 'drop shots' on such account. But this also implies then when one comes to positional (left-right) accuracy, there is no point in being 'absolutely accurate'. With the longer shots if one is accurate as to left-right to the nearest five yards then that is adequate since it is only half the likely random distance variations described and also will not 'drop a shot'. With the middle and shorter irons this limit should be tightened to ± one third of the distance variation. This is because such clubs are concerned with the direct approach to the pin where accuracy is all important.

Next we consider those Four Impact Imperatives related to such Practical Accuracy.

Practical accuracy as to square face

At impact the ball will travel in the direction established by the club face and at right angles to it. Consider this relating to three main varieties of shot: The Drive, The Mid-Iron (say 6-Iron), The Putt.

The Drive

I assume a drive of 200 yards ± ten yards and that the Practical Accuracy as to left-right should be half this deviation and within ± 5 yards. Now five yards at a distance of 200 yards corresponds to a club off-square angle of:

$$\frac{60^* \times 5}{200} = 1.5 \text{ degrees}$$

* This figure '60' will keep cropping up and relates to the fact that a 60 degree angle describes an arc length at the end of a radius which is about equal to the radius.

This tells us that at impact we must have the club face square as to ± 1.5 degrees if the probability is that the ball will come to rest within ± five yards of a theoretically perfect flight line.

The Mid (6) Iron

I assume a hit of 140 yards ± 10 yards and that the Ideal Practical Accuracy as to left-right will be one third this deviation and will be ± 3½ yards. This permissible deviation at a distance of 140 yards corresponds to a club off-square angle of:

$$\frac{60 \times 3\frac{1}{2}}{140} = 1.5 \text{ degrees}$$

The Putt

It is difficult to find the basis of realistic left-right accuracy of putts but I shall assume that a good professional expects to sink a five foot putt nine times out of ten.

The hole is just over four inches wide and the ball is 1.68 inches in diameter but we know that a ball which rolls over the side of the hole usually does not drop. Thus we have to take a smaller effective hole diameter and I suggest three inches diameter to be on the safe side. This means that the putt will (almost certainly) sink if it is hit to within ± 1½ inches of the centre of the hole. At a distance of five feet the corresponding angle is:

$$\frac{60 \times 1\frac{1}{2}}{60} = 1.5 \text{ degrees}$$

A generalisation

We can generalise about all the above calculations and state:

Good accuracy for any shot requires a club face which is square to ± 1½ degrees.

What does 'a degree' look like?

Most people have experience as to what some popular angles 'look like' by inspection judgment and especially as to:

90 degrees	a right angle
60 degrees	an equal-angle triangle
45 degrees	half a right angle

But how many people could tell the difference between one degree and two degrees?

Fig.4.1

To assist in such judgment, Fig. 4.1 gives all the degrees up to five in unit increments. In golf such fine angles have to be judged as to the angle of the squareness of the club sole which is typically about two and a half inches long at the sole edge (where squareness must be judged). The following table gives the correlation between angle and the difference in position of the club face at heel and toe. In other words, if one takes the club heel as a fixed reference point, then these distances are the amount by which the club toe is open (or closed).

Club face angle from true square	Toe-heel deviation distance
0	0
1 degree	1 millimetre
2 degrees	2 millimetres
3 degrees	3 millimetres
4 degrees	4 millimetres
5 degrees	5 millimetres

This means that for general distance shots we must be aware of what 1½ millimetres (1½°) over 2½ inches looks like as to out-of-square.
IT'S FINE STUFF!

A personal experiment

These limits are so fine one wonders if they are achievable. But they must be, otherwise professional golfers could not play to scratch and better figures. But how is it done?

I did some experiments. As an engineer I think I have a good eye for such concepts as to 'what is parallel?' and I laid out a line and by eye judged a second line some two inches away to 'be parallel'. I discovered that my accuracy was to about $1/6$th of a degree (.16 millimetre over the equivalent 2½ inch club face length). This was quite adequate to be in the correct league for the accuracies we are considering. But the problem in golf is that we have no datum line against which to judge parallelism or squareness. I don't know the answer to this problem because it would involve the concept that 'the mind's eye' was aware of some theoretical perfect line against which it could judge the squareness of a club face. What is clear is that the human psychic faculty is well adequate to *compare* parallelism and squareness when it has a comparison reference. But how could this be done (in golf) without such a specific datum? I think we have to settle for the thought that some people have the ability to establish a psychic reference as to perfect squareness.

Practical accuracy as to ball impact 'centrality'

I do not have any scientific information on the penalties for hitting the ball off the centre of the club although a golf machine could produce such figures and I hope the golf companies will do such trials. Here, for the moment, I rely on the experience of Mr Keith MacDonald, the professional at the Berkshire Club who tells me:

1   The requirement for centrality accuracy is much finer than people suppose and the good shot must impact within a ⅜ inch radius of the club centre.

2   Outside this, for a zone either side of a further ⅜ inch radius, there will be distinct loss of distance (due to centre of percussion twisting couples) and outside this again we are in the realm of thoroughly bad shots off toe and heel.

3   The same remarks also apply to vertical centrality in that if the ball is over ⅜ inch off centrality upwards it will 'sky' whilst similarly if it is below it will skim the ground. This effect is much mis-understood since some people think a 'skied' ball is due to hitting right underneath the ball, whereas it is only necessary to hit the ball so far off vertical club centre that at full ball compression the ball is not totally in normal contact with the club.

The result of such opinions, and Mr MacDonald is one of the best teaching professionals in Britain, is that we have an approximate idea of permitted tolerance in hitting the ball off centre. It is ⅜ inch, as shown in Fig. 4.2. This gives a 'sweet spot' of ¾ inch diameter.

This is a far finer tolerance than our Typical Golfer imagines is required and failure in this matter is a significant cause of lack of length. I suspect (confirmed by scientific tests – see later) that our Typical Golfer wanders over a club face radius of more like ¾ inch and thus is constantly in the club face zones where there is substantial loss of distance.

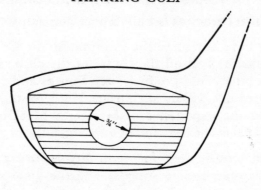

Fig.4.2

None of this has anything to do with golfing style but is simply a problem of repeating mechanical accuracy. One may have a 'perfect swing' and still be all over the course due to this lack of impact accuracy.

The practical accuracy for club direction of motion at impact (hooking and slicing)

If the club does not strike the ball with a direction which is in the line of intended flight, i.e. the club is cutting across the ball, then this produces a slice curling off to the right if the cutting-across is out-to-in. Similarly, a hook is produced by cutting-across the ball from in-to-out.

In both cases the phenomenon is due to the cutting-across – 'stroking' – the ball to produce spin about a vertical axis. With the slice the spin is clockwise and this means that the side of the ball nearer the player is moving faster than the remoter side and this creates extra air resistance on the near side which forces the ball off course to the right. A similar reason holds for the anti-clockwise spinning of the hooked ball.

Very little appears to be known about 'how much spin produces how much slice' (although it could easily be determined on an adjustable golfing machine) but from some rough calculation of my own and from talks with Mr Keith MacDonald, the Berkshire professional, I offer the following rough appraisal.

1   A mild slice occurs if the out-to-in direction is more than three degrees off a true line.*

2   A severe slice occurs if the out-to-in direction is more than six degrees off a true line.*

3   Comparative figures hold for hooking.

I have no exact proof of such figures but they are supported on the experiments (see later) with my robot testing device DOC in that this device is set to detect the above values and Mr MacDonald, who can hook or slice at will and to specific degrees, found that DOC was giving a true result.

This suggests that the avoidance of slicing and hooking (to a reasonable level) requires that we keep our impact line into the ball within (say) ± three degrees of the true line through the ball to the flag.

This is not a very fine tolerance and as viewed from ten inches behind the ball it means that the approach path must not be more than ½ inch out of line. This is shown in Fig.4.3.

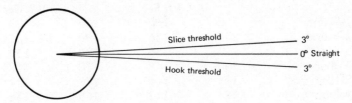

The practical accuracy requirement of club speed

For a given golf club, the distance the ball will go is

* These figures should be taken with caution

roughly proportional to the club speed at impact. I have made many measurements on this and there is little variation in the swing speed of a given golfer although there is great variation from golfer to golfer. Thus this is not a problem about which we can do much and it is more important to select the correct club from experience. However, my later tests show one very interesting matter and that is the extraordinary slowing down of the club if one hits the ground before the ball. I am not referring to 'digging-in' but merely firmly sliding along the ground for a few inches before impact. This can easily take 40 per cent off the club speed and ball yardage.

The remedial requirement is that given earlier as to the need to hit the ball with the centre of the club. The wrong effect is particularly noticeable with skied fairway wood shots. The skying shows one hit the ball too low but by the same token it is almost certain that the club was slowed due to ground friction.

Overall, the premium is on the clean impact but the accuracy requirement for this is greater than generally appreciated.

This table correlates club speed and distance:

| | Club Professional | | Typical Golfer | |
	Yards	Club Speed Ft. Sec.	Yards	Club Speed Ft. Sec.
1-Wood	260	160	200	123
2-Wood	240	156	190	121
3-Wood	220	150	180	119
4-Wood	200	148	170	118
2-Iron	185	146	170	117
3-Iron	175	142	165	116
4-Iron	165	138	155	115
5-Iron	155	135	145	114
6-Iron	145	132	135	112
7-Iron	135	128	125	110
8-Iron	125	125	115	108
9-Iron	115	122	105	107
10-Iron	100	118	90	106

I used in the construction of my golfing robot DOC as described later.

This table shows that at the top end (1-Wood) the professional can generate 30 per cent more club speed and yardage than the Typical Golfer but that at the lower end of the scale the difference is only about ten per cent. This, of course, is due to the professional not striving for maximum distance with the shorter clubs since there is no point in doing so and the matter is one for correct club selection.

Summary of accuracy requirements

We can thus summarise the accuracy requirements of the Four Impact Imperatives.

1st Imperative – Square Face
The club face must be square to the true line to the hole to within ± 1½ degrees.

2nd Imperative – Ball Centrality to Club Face
The ball must be struck within a radius of ⅜ inch (1 centimetre) of club face centrality.

3rd Imperative – Club Motional Direction at Impact
The club must come into the ball from a direction which is not more than three degrees (½ inch in ten inches) from the true line to the hole.

4th Imperative – Club Speed
If the ball is to travel as far as corresponds to the standard distance related to club selection, such as shown in the Table, then it must be struck *cleanly* and also in accordance with all the above Three Impact Imperatives.

5
The Five Laws of Cussedness

The whole point of golf is to hit the ball in a straight line and also to hit it very accurately as to direction. The only comparable games to require such straightness and directional accuracy are billiards and croquet. My reader may remember the game of croquet described in *Alice in Wonderland* in which flamingoes were used for mallets and hedgehogs for croquet balls. We shall see that the predicament of the human golfer is not too far from such a state of affairs.

Now there is nothing simpler than to construct an inanimate golfing machine which could probably beat any world champion. For it would meet those Four Impact Imperatives with ease by being a simple powered vertical-plane pendulum in a rigid mounting.

But the human golfer is not a simple vertical pendulum. He can become a sort of pendulum but one which is partly vertical and partly side-swiping. Furthermore, he has a far from rigid 'mounting' and is full of universal joints and elasticities so that he can sway in three directions at once!

The human being is far more flexible, intelligent and adaptable than a golfing machine and a given person can, for example:

Play twenty different games
Thread a needle
Paint a picture
Climb a mountain
Drive a motor-car or pilot an aeroplane.

This flexibility implies that a human being is a *general purpose* computer-performer. But when a game such as golf requires that he imitates a precise and rigid machine then he is at a disadvantage to that machine. A good analogy of the situation is the man who tries to draw a straight line on a piece of paper without using a ruler . . . it is impossible! A man can draw an approximate straight line or a circle or an equal-angled triangle but it will only be very approximate and cannot compare to what he could do with the mechanical aids of ruler, compasses and set-square. But when, in addition, a human golfer is supposed to hit a straight ball with a club which is describing an arc in a side-swipe plane which is neither horizontal nor vertical but at some unknown angle of plane, then he has real problems.

> *By all logical standards, golf is an impossible game for human beings and is certainly as difficult as Alice-in-Wonderland playing croquet with flamingoes for mallets.*

Nevertheless, we are stuck with the game (and I am certainly hooked) and thus the scientific problem is:

> *Exactly how are human golfers so inferior to a simple golfing machine which has no such problems?*

Laws of Cussedness

I have described earlier those Four Impact Imperatives which are so easy to design into an inanimate golfing machine with which the human golfer cannot compete and thus one asks 'what has that golfing machine got which I have not got?' Perhaps that is not the full formulation of the problem which may be in two parts:

1   What has the golfing machine got which I have not got?

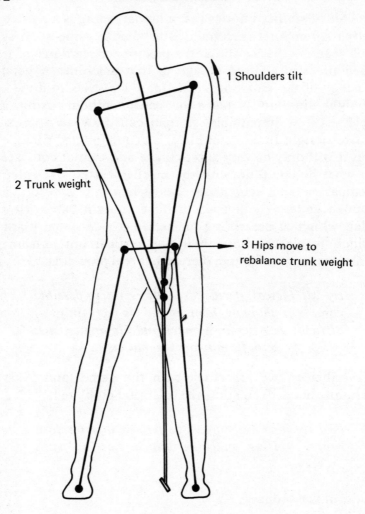

1 Shoulders tilt

2 Trunk weight

3 Hips move to rebalance trunk weight

Fig.5.1

2   What have I got that the golfing machine has not got and which appears to be to my human golfing disadvantage?

Now that's better! What the human being has (related to the second of the above pair of questions) are Five Laws of Cussedness. These are:

The First Law of Cussedness – Hand Asymmetry
The Second Law of Cussedness – Ground Arc
The Third Law of Cussedness – Jelly-on-Springs
The Fourth Law of Cussedness – Wrist-Cocking with Arm Rolling
The Fifth Law of Cussedness – Mental Stretch in a Complex System

The First Law of Cussedness – Hand Asymmetry

To impart power into a golf ball requires that both hands are firmly holding the club grip. But (for right-handed golfers) this means that we have to hold the club with the right hand about three inches lower than the left.

From the start this fact distorts the golfer's natural standing symmetry since either the left shoulder has to be higher than the right or alternatively the left shoulder has to be withdrawn whilst the right shoulder moves forwards towards the ball. In the latter case the golfer will almost certainly play a slicing shot with the right arm dominating round the right shoulder. But even if he takes up the preferred correction (see Fig. 5.1) by tilting the shoulders rather than twisting them, this will still create a basic asymmetry and distortion of his posture. A thoughtful golfer would have arranged that his parents ensured that he was born with a right arm some three inches longer than his left.

The best correction for this problem is given in chapter 22.

The Second Law of Cussedness – Ground Arc

A golfing machine is best made, is simplest made, as a powered pendulum swinging in a vertical plane so that its swing arc is in the same plane as the desired direction of ball flight. Thus it is producing an impact with the

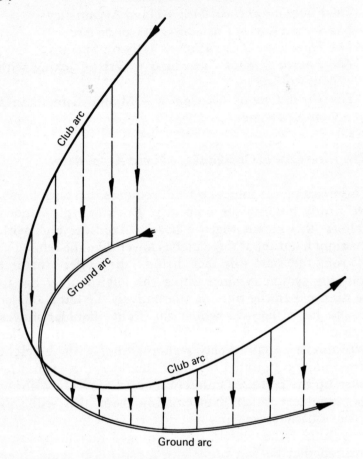

Fig. 5.2

ball which has no velocity component cutting across the ball. Such a golfing machine has no slicing or hooking problems. It is, as it were, swinging between its legs. But the human golfer has to stand at one side of the ball to give it a sideswipe in a plane which is typically 40 degrees from the vertical and this has a ground arc component (of a radius of about 110 inches). This means that at only one point of that ground arc is the club travelling in the correct direction towards the hole. This critical point may be called the Tangential Point but if one hits the ball before this then one has an in-to-out strike which produces a hook and if one hits after this critical point then one has an out-to-in strike which produces a slice.

It is a veritable Law of Cussedness and one would *never* design a golfing machine on such side-swiping geometry with its critical curving ground arc as shown in Fig.5.2.

The Third Law of Cussedness – Jelly-on-Springs

A golfing machine can perform flawlessly because it has a rigid basic frame to act as a fixed datum for its mechanics. By contrast, the human being is full of devices (for his adaptability) which ensure his ability to move in complex patterns in all three space directions. The main features are the following joints as shown in Fig.5.3.

1	Neck joint	8	Right hip joint
2	Right shoulder joint	9	Left hip joint
3	Left shoulder joint	10	Right knee joint
4	Right elbow joint	11	Left knee joint
5	Left elbow joint	12	Right ankle joint
6	Right wrist joint	13	Left ankle joint
7	Left wrist joint	14	Spine joints

There are fourteen major joints in the human body (and I leave out the smaller joints of fingers and toes) which vary in their characteristics from being simple hinges such as the knees to being full universal joints such as the hips. The permutations of possible actions and postures in the human body are virtually limitless. But whilst this is an advantage towards physical adaptability it also means that the golfer cannot imitate a simple golfing machine. Man, as a golfer, is like a Rolls

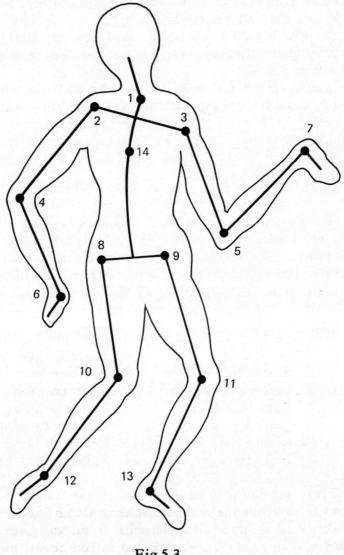

Fig.5.3

Royce trying to behave like a Ford, and his very adaptability makes him a virtual Jelly-on-Springs.

The Fourth Law of Cussedness – Wrist-Cocking with Arm Rolling

A golfing machine uses a single powered lever whereas the golfer uses a two-link lever system, the first link being his arms and the second link being the club. But this system is hinged at the wrists and so the golfer has to use a flailing swing which is much more complex than the single lever swing of the golfing machine.

But this of itself is not such a defect, since a flail action is quite efficient and effective. But where the trouble lies is in the fact that the wrists can hinge in two different planes, producing:

Wrist-Hinging: that motion of the wrists in swinging a golf club which is in the same arc as the whole swing and which preserves the club face square to that arc. With such a wrist-hinging action one automatically comes square into the ball.

Wrist-Cocking: that motion of the wrists in swinging a golf club which is at right angles to the main swing arc and which, if the club head is to stay on the main swing plane involves rolling the arms and thus taking the club face away from that desirable squareness to the swing arc.

Experiment (see Fig. 5.4)
1   Address the ball with a club in the normal fashion.
2   Cock the wrists by about 40 degrees so that the club head is raised from the ground and is horizontal.
3   Bring the club head back onto the swing arc by rolling the arms clockwise. It will be seen that the club face is now lying along the swing arc instead of square to it.

Now although the above experiment has been done at ground level in the ball zone, exactly the same situation takes place at the top of the backswing if one allows the wrists to cock. This is due to the fact that the momentum of the club towards the top of the backswing

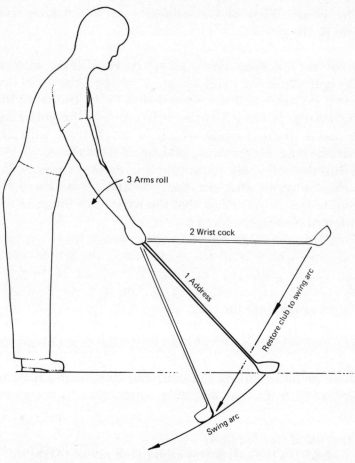

3 Arms roll

2 Wrist cock

1 Address

Restore club to swing arc

Swing arc

Fig.5.4

keeps the club moving and this drags the wrists into
cocking whilst causing the arms to roll. This phenomenon can easily be observed by noting the position of the
club face at the top of the backswing. If the toe of the
club is pointing to the ground then the club face must
have rotated completely off square and is now lying
along the club arc. There is a second alternative danger
in that if the backswing is very slow there will be little
residual momentum in the club head towards the top of

the swing and thus the wrists may cock without arm rolling, in which case the club head 'loops' out of the original swing plane and the club comes over the golfer's head. This is disastrous since it would require a skew downswing plane to get the club head back to the ball.

But the normal phenomenon is the one first described in that the wrist-cocking produces arm rolling and takes the club well off desirable squareness and in the downswing a reverse operation has to take place but with some uncertainty as to success.

We shall see in chapter 20 that it could be highly desirable to limit the backswing to pure hinging of the wrists as defined earlier, thus ensuring the club face is always square to the swing arc.

The Fifth Law of Cussedness – Mental Stretch in a Complex System

The problem of the golfer is how to achieve those Four Impact Imperatives within a system containing the Four Laws of Cussedness just described. In chapter 2 we noted that golf is a systems problem rather than a machine problem, but this system is quite complex and the golfer has only his experience and mental faculties to try and cope with it. But the degree of complexity is such that this fact alone introduces a Fifth Law of Cussedness related to the possible inability of our minds to control the system. It is a problem of Mental Stretch. Human beings only have a certain degree of mental stretch, the ability to keep a complexity of ideas in focus, and even this is highly variable from moment to moment. How often are we given a telephone number or a name or an address only to be totally unable to remember it within a matter of seconds.

The effect is particularly noticeable on the golf course in the way in which we may complete a round with a certain amount of mental grip on the game. But the following round may well start very badly until we gradually remember what we were doing right in the previous round.

The problem of Mental Stretch *can* be dealt with by a combination of simplification and condensation of ideas and this is dealt with in Part 3 on Psycho-Golf.

But overall we have to face the fact that the problem of Mental Stretch in a Complex System is a Law of Cussedness in its own right.

Summary of The Five Laws of Cussedness

The First Law of Cussedness is due to the fact that we have to take the right hand grip lower than the left hand grip and this introduces a basic asymmetry and distortion into the body posture.

The Second Law of Cussedness is that the human golfer has to take a side-swipe at the ball so that the club is moving in an arc related to the ground and only one point of this arc points in the correct flight direction.

The Third Law of Cussedness is due to the multiplicity of joints in the human skeleton which permit 'postural wander' to the degree of Jelly-on-Springs.

The Fourth Law of Cussedness is due to the fact that the wrists can hinge in two directions at right angles to each other and the wrist-cocking mode creates arm rolling which has the club face along the swing plane instead of square to it.

The Fifth Law of Cussedness is that the golfer is in danger of running out of Mental Stretch in trying to control the inherent complexity of the systematic situation.

Thus the problem of the golfer is:

How to meet Four Impact Imperatives in the presence of Five Laws of Cussedness?

6
Golf Opinion

The golfing machine limits itself to actualising those Four Golfing Imperatives as to:

1 Square face
2 Central strike
3 In-line direction of club at impact
4 Correct club speed

Having actualised these four simple matters it can then play to scratch or better.

But the human golfer is not a machine but an ill co-ordinated *system*, suffering from the adverse mathematics of System Reliability Laws which are in turn aggravated by those Five Laws of Cussedness.

How does that Typical Golfer cope with such unfair odds? He turns the game into a myth whose chief features are subjective opinions. Let us imagine that a golfer has struck a bad patch and he is unwise enough to seek counsel from ten other golfers who have recently been playing with him. He asks them, 'What am I doing wrong?' The sort of opinions he will receive are:

1 'There is no doubt that you are hitting from the top'
2 'Watch that sway, old man'
3 'Of course, you don't really pivot, you know'
4 'It's all in the mind. You have to attack the ball with real determination'

5   'Relax. Take it easy. You are over-anxious'
6   'Although your main fault is slicing, you really
       have a hooker's grip. Try hanging onto the club
       at the top of the backswing'
7   'Eye on the ball, that's the real golf secret'
8   'Try to imagine you have two planes of glass
       round your neck: one for the backswing and one
       for the downswing and that the two planes are ten
       degrees apart'
9   'Stand closer to the ball'
10   'Stand further away from the ball'

Golf opinion dominates the game and that is not
unreasonable. If one cannot master the game it makes
sense to turn it into a mythical dream in which it is the
opinions which count. At least one can get some good
conversation out of the matter. One may even buoy
oneself up for the next round on the principle that 'it is
better to travel hopefully than to arrive'.

The origin of the myth of 'The Secret of Golf'

Just occasionally a golfer develops a consistent feature of
bad play which becomes an obsession with him so that
any way of dispensing with this particular feature must
surely be 'the secret of golf'. Such a consistent feature of
bad golf is almost sure to be the result of some
maladjustment of one of those fourteen large joints of
the human body each of which has several modes of
motion. But somehow, and perhaps more by luck than
design, the golfer finds that if he makes an adjustment
with one or other of his fourteen main joints, then that
bad feature seems to disappear as though by magic. This
adjustment can only be 'the secret of golf', to be
compared with the 'Open Sesame' of Ali Baba and the
Forty Thieves. However, such golf secrets will only last
for a couple of days since those Five Laws of Cussedness

are not to be defeated by such a facile formula. Unfortunately, before the elapse of that time, our Typical Golfer will have told the whole club about the 'secret of golf', only to be faced with the sorry conclusion the next day that his secret does not work at all.

I have to confess that in the past I have been a master purveyor of golf secrets only to suffer in anguish as they slipped away from me into total ineffectiveness.

I decided that the time had arrived for sober reflections.

7
Sober Reflections

The pundits of the golfing world divide themselves into two groups in a very interesting fashion.

1 The Analysts of Technique This is the school of thought which considers that the game of golf can be played well by attention to detail related to the significant different *mechanical* aspects of the game. On the whole this present book is in harmony with this approach but the danger is that there is a lunatic fringe who may consider that there is some single 'secret of golf'.

2 The 'Naturalists' The Naturalist school of thought considers that in each of us there is a Natural Golfer and that our problem is to 'relax' and let that Natural Golfer take over. It tends to view the golf stroke 'as a whole' and that one either has the right feel for the game or not. I sympathise with this point of view which has a legitimate basis in organic theory in that 'the whole is more than the sum of the parts', but I confess that it has never worked for me.

On balance I come down decidedly on the side of the Analysts because of my dedication to the reality of those Five Laws of Cussedness which demand *technique* for their subjugation. It is all very well talking about 'relaxing' and 'playing naturally' but this simply will not prevent one slicing or shanking and the rest of the sins to which the golfer is heir.

I am not saying that there is not a good time to forget about rules and techniques but in the longer run one will only play consistent golf if one adheres to them. Whenever one makes a bad shot there must be a *reason* for it, a reason related to the fact that we find it difficult to imitate that simple golfing machine, the mechanical powered pendulum.

Somewhere and somehow we must be playing ducks-and-drakes with Newton's Laws of Motion for golf is a game played strictly inside the limits of rigorous physical laws. It is true that there is a very small minority, the 'natural ball players', who can get away with murder and escape the Rule Book. But for each one of these there are ten times as many golfers who cannot perform in such a carefree fashion and succeed.

Today, for example, I was playing very badly with consistent slicing and I tried 'forgetting about the Rule Book' and letting the Natural Golfer in me (all fifty years of it) take over in a natural fashion. The result was disastrous and only when I remembered to 'stand up properly' did my game recover.

I do not suggest for one moment that our Typical Golfer can play consistently by adhering to the Rule Book. This is because our fourteen universal joints can at any time introduce the most remarkable deviations into our swing and its accuracy. But in the long run, only taking thought about the matter in an analytical fashion can get us back on the rails.

It is certainly true that there are times when we find ourselves playing consistently badly, perhaps our drives are being reduced to 150 yards, and we cannot imagine what on earth has gone wrong. But this is a mental failure and one has to put up with it until one's mental resource thinks properly again about fundamentals.

Let me summarise the ideas so far in this book:

1   Golf, as played by human beings, is a *systems* problem and comes under the Laws of System

Reliability (really 'Unreliability') in that the Typical
Golfer may be 98 per cent efficient as to each of
(say) six vital components of the game but this
leaves him with an overall system reliability of only
about 88 per cent and thus he must drop about nine
shots in the round, even allowing for his Proper Par.

2   A simple golfing machine can be constructed to
play to a handicap of scratch. But the Typical
Golfer cannot emulate this, perhaps because of Five
Laws of Cussedness, notably:

a)   Hand asymmetry at the grip.
b)   The swing is a horizontal arc at impact.
c)   The human being is a Jelly-on-Springs.
d)   Wrist-cocking and arm rolling take the club
face off squareness.
e)   Excessive mental stretch in a complex system.

The problem of System Reliability (1) dominates the
whole situation and our problem is that we combine two
or three minor faults at any time and it is *the sum of the
faults* rather than any single specific fault. But human
beings like to rationalise and oversimplify and if we have
a bad shot we like to attribute it to a single cause such
as:

'I did not pivot properly'
'Swaying again!'
'Hitting from the top!'
'Lost my balance'
    . . . and you name it.

But I was developing a scientific hunch that such
diagnoses only contained a germ of truth and that the
reality might be that we were dropping shots because:

*The (say) six vital factors were in a state of flux
and combination and thus any simple specific
analysis was invalid*

Typically, I imagined that a bad shot might well be due

to having three different things wrong by only a little but that their cumulative effect was disaster. If this were true then we had no adequate method of analysing the situation and correcting it since I had never met a teaching golf professional who would make such a complex announcement as:

> 'Madam, your bad shot was due to just a teeny
> bit of closed-face combined with just a soupçon
> of sway and the merest trace of overswinging,
> not to mention your anxious emotional state!'

And yet, as an engineer who had studied systems reliability, I knew that this sort of analysis was typical of how one must measure the true performance of a *system* and that usually there is 'no villain in the piece' but just an accumulation of slightly off-colour vital components.

This thing required *science* and I told myself: 'Get thee to a laboratory!'

PART TWO
New Experimental Data

8
DOC

Let me recap. I had suspected that golfers' problems were not due to some 'Chief Defect' but were due to an accumulation of small errors and that if these were to be correctly analysed it would need laboratory measurement. I was faced with a preliminary dilemma as to whether I should consider:

a)   Measuring what the golfer does, or
b)   Knowing the correct mechanics of a straight stroke (that golfing machine), measuring deviations from this i.e. measuring the Four Impact Imperatives.

I decided that the second was the correct course since I had seen golfers produce good results with a great variety of individual styles and that to 'measure the golfer' would take me into an impossible jungle of variations. But when it comes to 'measuring the impact of club with ball' the Four Impact Imperatives were well known:

1   The face of the club must be square.
2   The club must contact the ball at the centre of percussion which, for practical purposes, is also the centre of the club.
3   The club must be moving in the direction of required flight if spin is to be avoided (slices and hooks).
4   It would be useful to know the club speed at impact since there was a known correlation between this and yardage.

These four factors are the basis of the measuring Robot I
designed which is named DOC.

The Specification of 'DOC'

I called my robot DOC because it was to be an automatic
electronic diagnostic system and DOC was to measure
what happened at impact with the ball as regards the
above four main features.

Fortunately, I had the necessary experience of photo-
electronic logical systems to be able to conceive the
design without much apprehension.

For those technically interested, the features of 'DOC'
(see Figs. 8.1 and 8.3 in the section of photographs) are
based on the following principles. In all cases the golfer
was to swing at an actual or celluloid ball. A lamp above
creates a shadow of the clubhead in the impact zone and
below the striking mat is an array of photocells.

1   *Square face of club*
This is done by an array of photocells (A, B, C of
Fig.8.2) in that when the club shadow reaches A the
other cells are interrogated:

    a)   If cells B and C are dark then the club face must
        be SHUT.
    b)   If cells B and C are both illuminated then the
        club face must be OPEN.
    c)   If cell C is dark but cell B is illuminated then the
        club face is about square.

The degree of differentiation was an angle of 6 degrees
from correct squareness but this was adjustable.

2   *Central Impact*
This is monitored by photocells E and J. If E stays
illuminated during impact the club shadow must have
passed inboard (towards the golfer) and the ball must
have been hit off the TOE. Conversely if the photocell J

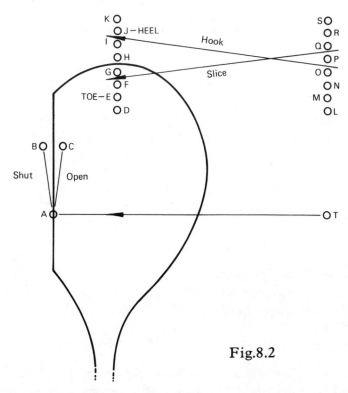

Fig.8.2

is darkened during impact then the club head shadow must have passed over it and the ball must have been hit off the HEEL.

The two photocells E and J are each located one half inch either side of the ideal central strike line and thus DOC indicates a TOE or HEEL strike outside these limits.

3 Slicing and hooking

Slicing or hooking is monitored by the two arrays of eight photocells D to K and L to S. The photocells in each array are located one-fifth of an inch apart whilst the two arrays are six inches apart. This means that a line of strike which crosses a line joining opposite cells in each array is an angular strike error averaging 2 degrees. Similarly, a greater angularity as to opposite photocells establishes directional faults of 4, 6, 8, . . . degrees.

The measuring electronics is set to fault the golfer if his strike direction is more than 4 degrees from the true.

4 *Ball Yardage*

Ball yardage is calculated from measuring the club head shadow speed as between the two photocells T and A. The accurate formula of the Golfing Society is man-ipulated mathematically to give a display of ball yardage as to estimated carry and roll. A switch (see Fig. 8.3) enables the golfer to choose the correct calibration for five woods and five irons:

1-Wood (8 ounce head)	3-Iron
1-Wood (7 ounce head)	5-Iron
1-Wood (6 ounce head)	7-Iron
3-Wood	9-Iron
5-Wood	Pitching Wedge

The significance of making provision for different head weights for the 1-Woods will become clearer later in the book. We found there were two sorts of golfer, one who gets better yardage with light clubs and one who gets better yardage with heavier clubs.

5 *Statistical Display of Faults*

DOC displays six faults:

HOOK	SLICE	swing direction
OPEN	SHUT	club face aspect
TOE	HEEL	ball on club face

As the golfer uses DOC these faults cause digital displays to wink the fault concerned and as successive strokes are taken the faults are totalised on the same digital displays. Thus at the end of (say) ten strokes it is obvious which is one's worst fault or pattern of faults. A typical result might be:

Fault	Number of Faults
HOOK	7
SLICE	0
OPEN	1
SHUT	3
TOE	0
HEEL	1

From the above it is clear that the golfer's problem is hooking with a secondary tendency to a shut club face which will create a duck-hook. The other small faults can be ignored as insignificant.

6 Strike Efficiency

DOC keeps a tally of the total number of fault-free strokes and compares these with the number of swings taken and the ratio is displayed as the STRIKE EFFICIENCY. From this, using a table, one can get quite a close idea of the golfer's true handicap.

DOC Goes Into Production

My experiments using the early development model of DOC took place during 1976-78 and I had no intention for this equipment except as a research tool to illuminate the game of golf. But a friend of mine who is both golfer and business-man considered that DOC had a commercial selling future, pre-eminently in Japan where land is so scarce that even golf driving-ranges use stopping nets. I expect it will be advertised, but in the meantime I will be happy to reply to enquiries sent to me at the address on page viii.

This production model is shown in Fig. 8.3.

9

The First Trials of DOC

I had mentioned to the Dunlop Sports Co. that I proposed to build DOC, and at a lunch with Mr F. F. Picken of the Dunlop Company on 22 October 1975 I had rashly promised that I could build DOC in eight weeks flat. This was rash because there would be some special electronic computing functions involved which I had never tackled before. Fortunately my friend Dr Henry Kemhadjian of Southampton University drew the appropriate circuits for me on the back of an envelope and these worked first time. So DOC was finished in seven weeks with time to spare.

The very first tests were made by myself with DOC in the open air in my back garden and although DOC worked perfectly, the results were not too flattering to my personal golfing prospects. The first ten swings recorded the following traumatic results:

Swing 1	No faults
Swing 2	Heel hit
Swing 3	Heel hit
Swing 4	Face open
Swing 5	Mild slice, face open, toe hit
Swing 6	Face open
Swing 7	Toe hit
Swing 8	Heel hit
Swing 9	Face open
Swing 10	Heel hit

Now what does the reader make of that? I concluded that

my golf could only be described as eccentric and that my problem was *variability*. Clearly DOC was going to be an interesting device and it certainly had my face red on those first private tests. Fortunately, it started to snow so I bundled the equipment back into my garage where there is hardly room to swing a cat let alone a golf club. In spite of that fact my golfing friend Mr Oickle managed to clock-up about 200 yards on DOC under conditions in which I feared he might break his arms. This stood as a 'record' for two weeks.

By this time my buddies at the Berkshire Golf Club had heard about my little exploit and at a committee meeting it was resolved to invite DOC into the club for the amusement of members and perhaps I might also learn something useful myself. Still in my garage, DOC had been tested by Keith MacDonald, the Berkshire professional, and his two assistants at that time, Gordon and Graham. Now Gordon is a long hitter with a tendency to hit the ball on the downswing and he managed to take a 'divot' out of DOC and scattered parts of its strike-mat all round my garage. However, he was not only contrite about the incident but provided the material for a new strike-mat from a bit of old conveyor belting and this proved the long-wearing answer to DOC strike-mats.

A little later some of the committee of the Berkshire, including Dr Stanhope Furber, the President, visited DOC in the confined premises of my garage and having made some swings pronounced that DOC would be invited into the club, providing it was arranged that it could only be used under the control of selected people. This involved me in fitting DOC with a key switch and the two keys were handed over to the club secretary, Walter Seabrook, and to our professional Keith Mac-Donald.

The first weekend trials at the Berkshire

With DOC duly installed in an excellent upper games-
room at the Berkshire with plenty of swinging room and
a high ceiling, I had offered to be in attendance over the
weekend in January 1976. Something like a hundred
golfers, including lady golfers, must have swung through
DOC. My first impression was one of horror since
certain golfers were coming within a few inches of
striking the high projector lamp at the end of wild
follow-throughs. I had to close down the trials hastily,
and increase the lamp height to over eight feet, which
gave a safe margin.

On that flrst weekend there was a notable result. Some
golfers were so fascinated by the yardage which DOC
could display that they swung fully-out disregarding the
winking red lights as to faults they were incurring and I
realised that DOC must be revised to inflict yardage
penalties on those who forced power without regard to
accuracy.

Dunlop visit DOC

I had told Dunlop about DOC being operational at the
Berkshire and Mr Picken, the Sports managing director,
and Mr Haines, their technical manager, came down on
30 January 1976 and generally approved of DOC. In
particular they insisted that I introduce no new features
(I had had in mind two more) but that the important
matter was to make the display unambiguous and simple.
After their inspection of DOC we went out for sixteen
holes on the Blue Course in freezing weather and I was
beaten five and three by Mr Picken but was consoled by
Mr Haines' offer to pull my trolley. The course was so
frozen that it was possible to reach the greens by
bouncing balls over bunkers and I think I was beaten
because Mr Picken latched onto this bizarre technique

before I realised what was happening. Back at the bar, we worked out the next procedure since Dunlop was definitely interested in DOC. It was agreed that DOC would go to the Liverpool testing ground of Dunlop where Neil Coles would drive balls and compare the yardage with what DOC pronounced.

In the meantime the experience at the Berkshire had shown up about six minor electronic problems and I decided to give DOC quite a re-build before taking it to Liverpool.

But overall, the experience of about four weeks at the Berkshire had been very interesting in a number of respects. In the first place it had shown that a golfer could really diagnose himself as to his 'main faults' and that a golfer might take DOC's advice where he might not be convinced by a teaching golf professional. Typically, DOC might show that a given golfer was consistently hitting the ball too near to the club heel and that was *fact*. Another matter which became clear was that most golfers exaggerate their yardage by some ten to twenty per cent and that is because when they pace their drives they do not allow for the fact that the human pace is usually less than one yard.

But a further aspect of the DOC demonstrations was the extraordinary accuracy of the professionals in avoiding 'faults' and Keith MacDonald could score 'no faults' nine times out of ten whereas the typical club golfer had about one fault nine times out of ten. I began to consider that the difference between the pro golfer and the amateur would be found in the realm of *consistent precision*. DOC indicated that the desirable degree of such precision was in the realms of 'the nearest ¼ inch' and yet amateur golfers were taking no precautions to achieve such fine limits of accuracy.

Another odd aspect was that the better amateurs at The Berkshire could swing faster and theoretically hit a ball farther than the professionals but they could not combine this with the consistent 'no fault' accuracy.

Finally, another odd aspect. I had assumed in my calibration of DOC as to speed-yardage that each club would be swung at the same speed. But a series of tests with one of the club assistant professionals showed conclusively that the higher-numbered iron clubs were swung 30 per cent slower than the woods. I had suspected this, but now we were getting *facts*.

The second trials of DOC

The second round of trials with DOC was to be at the Dunlop premises at Speke near Liverpool where they have a testing ground including a golf driving machine and a laid out ground area which is marked with tapes every ten yards of distance.

The trials were to be held on 1 April 1976 with Mr Neil Coles driving the balls and the main objective was to confirm or otherwise the speed calibration which was based on a 260 yards 1-Wood drive for a club speed of 160 ft per second. DOC had been transported to Liverpool in a station-wagon and had travelled via the Dunlop research department at Barnsley in Yorkshire and thus might have been quite a bit shaken about. So I went to Liverpool with an extra day in hand before the trials to check that everything was in working order and I had a bag full of soldering irons, wire and electronic parts just in case. In the event, when DOC was assembled it worked first time and was no worse for its travels.

However, one thing concerned me and that was that DOC was designed to work indoors and its photocells were not adjusted for outdoor daylight operation and neither was the equipment weatherproofed to operate in rain. But the Dunlop test chief at Speke, Mr Michael Shaw, told me that 'it never rains during tests' although as he spoke those words to me it was raining quite hard. I had my fingers crossed for the following day.

The Dunlop personnel and I, who had come up for the tests, were staying at the Holiday Inn in Liverpool and on the night of the 31 March we had a phone call from Neil Coles that he was delayed in Birmingham but that he would be up the following morning in time. On the actual day we gathered in the hall of the Holiday Inn at about 8.45 am to find Neil Coles waiting for us so the party was complete and we all went off to Dunlop at Speke. We spent the first hour in a boardroom where, with chalk and blackboard, I explained to those present how DOC worked and I had many penetrating questions from Mr Coles. It was agreed that the tests would consist of:

> Yardage with 1-Wood as to actual distances and
>   DOC instrumented distances.
> Yardage as above but with 5-Iron
> Yardage as above but with 9-Iron
> Club speed with 1-Wood as determined by DOC.

In each case Mr Coles would strike six balls and we would average the three furthest. The results were:

	Mr Coles' yardage	DOC yardage
1-Wood	285	283
5-Iron	170	170
9-Iron	123	120

In addition Mr Coles' swing speed was determined as 180 feet per second. All the values were remarkably close and since DOC did not take notice of wind or terrain, then the agreement was sufficient to declare that the DOC calibration was accurate enough and did not need to be changed. I was very interested in Mr Coles' swing speed of 180 feet per second which was considerably faster than the 'standard' professional swing speed of 160 feet per second, but he certainly secured the extra yardage to go with it.

Ten blind swings with DOC

Early random use of DOC showed that it would not give useful results unless it was used in some methodical fashion. If used as a fun-thing on a random swinging basis, then it was a 60-minute wonder but afterwards people lost interest. But I was convinced that DOC could be used as a serious teaching aid and to realise this aim we established a procedure:

1   The DOC display of information would be covered up by a blind (we later used a switch).
2   The golfer under test would take ten swings while an observer peeped behind the blind and recorded on paper what had happened.
3   At the end of the ten swings, we would take out averages and rate faults in numerical extent of occurences.
4   The golfer would be told his chief faults and also those departments of his game which were OK.

Many such tests were taken but I will quote only two in detail as follows:

Mr A (about 45 years old – 12 handicap)

RESULTS

Swing No.	Yardage 1-Wood	Faults
1	224	
2	240	
3	182	Mild toe hit – Open face
4	245	
5	254	
6	257	
7	218	Loss of club speed due to clouting strike mat
8	186	Mild toe hit – Open face
9	249	
10	195	Mild toe hit

The results were then summarised as:

    Yardage (average of best three) .....253 yards
    3 faults – mild toe hit
    2 faults – open face
    1 fault – clouting strike mat
    Zero faults – 6 out of 10

Now what this showed was that Mr A. was generally a good golfer with a long hit but that he was erratic in his ball impact, with a tendency to combine hitting towards the toe with an open face. He fully agreed this diagnosis and put his thinking cap on. Clearly it was a rather tricky problem since six out of ten swings were perfect and thus it would be wrong to make any major change of style. My own reading of the matter was related to the fact that in the first six swings there was only one double-fault whereas in the last four swings there were three faults. I diagnosed the matter as 'loss of attention and fatigue' towards the end of the test and that in future we should allow more waiting time between swings. On an actual golf course there is an average time lapse between successive shots of about three minutes whilst we were using DOC at about 45 second intervals.

Mrs U (about 30 years old – scratch)

RESULTS
Swing No.	Yardage 1-Wood	Faults
1	197	
2	197	
3	161	Mild heel hit
4	205	
5	195	Slight strike-mat clout
6	204	
7	211	
8	220	
9	210	
10	202	

Yardage (average of best three) .....214 yards
1 fault – mild heel hit
1 fault – slight strike-mat clout
Zero faults – 8 out of 10

Now I had agreed with Keith MacDonald that any given single fault out of ten swings can have no significance and this meant that Mrs U was playing *perfect women's golf* both as regards faults and yardage. We told her so and she was rather pleased as she had been suffering from a little loss of confidence. The next day* she went out and won the Berkshire County Ladies Championship with the match play scores:

6 and 5
6 and 5
7 and 6
4 and 3

There are no prizes for guessing the identity of Mrs U. Now what was interesting about Mrs U's ten swings was that the last five were quite flawless and yet she was swinging at rapid intervals and this contrasted with Mr A. It suggests that the extra strength of men is due to an aggressive release of adrenalin which quickly exhausts itself and which does not occur with women. This may account for the tendency of the ladies to get their distance by a big mild swing rather than a swing-hit. It also suggests that male golfers may be very sensitive to fatigue and can suddenly go off form in the middle of a round. It would even suggest that male golfers should be careful not to use up their adrenalin flow by walking too fast between shots.

The interesting comment by Mr W

Mr W took seven swings on DOC almost by accident. He was visiting the Berkshire Club with a society and I

---

*A month later she reached the final of the English Women's Championship.

In 1977 she became British Women's Champion.

happened to be having a drink with two members of our Committee when one of them said: 'There's a young man you should try out on DOC.' No sooner said than done and Mr W (scratch) got his driver and spiked shoes and we all went off upstairs to give Mr W the Blind Test. His swing distance was prodigious, between 280 and 290 yards and with negligible faults. But after seven swings he made the following comment.

Because the tests were indoors we were using a celluloid ball and this was absorbing negligible energy at impact so that the club follow-through was occurring at full swing speed instead of dropping (say) 30 per cent of speed at impact. Now as Mr W was swinging at his top speed, this fact was throwing him a little off balance during the follow-through.

The result could only be that we had to find a new sort of practice ball which would absorb energy.

However, this result suggested that practice swings without a ball may be totally misleading and although they may be useful for 'warming up', they should not be considered as serious practice swings.

10

DOC Diagnoses Types of Golfer

So far in this book I have analysed aspects of golf as being common to all golfers. But observing golfers in action I had noted many different styles of playing. Dr David Williams in his book *The Science of The Golf Swing* (Pelham Books) has strongly advocated the use of much lighter clubs than normal and down to five-ounce head weights but swung faster.

I considered that with DOC and its ability to measure swing speeds with accuracy it might be possible to throw light on these matters. I arranged with the International Sports Company to make up five otherwise identical 1-Woods with R shafts but with head weights of 6, 7, 8, 9, and 10 ounces. These are shown in Fig. 10.1 (in the section of photographs) with a further five clubs which I later used with a fixed head weight of seven ounces but with shafts of different whippiness. I then called on my golfing friends at the Berkshire to volunteer to find out what their swing speeds were (in feet per second) against this wide variation of club head weights. Altogether ten golfers (three women) collaborated.

The results were bizarre for I immediately found that there were three distinct groups of golfers characterised by:

Speed Golfers Such golfers were able to swing the lighter clubs with increasing speeds and get increasing yardages down to the six ounce head club and with the swing speed and yardage curves still rising as shown in Fig.

10.2. Such golfers supported Dr Williams' advocacy of lighter clubs.

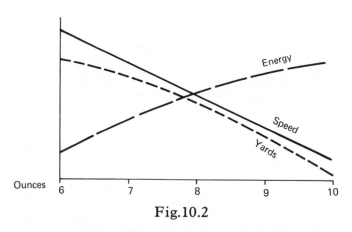

Fig.10.2

Power Golfers But there was another group of golfers with just about the opposite characteristics. They could not swing the six ounce club much faster than the eight ounce and they appeared to have a relatively fixed swing speed irrespective of club head weight. But such golfers could greatly increase the measured power into the club head with increasing club head weight as shown in Fig. 10.3. Such golfers could not take advantage of Dr Williams' advocacy of lighter clubs.

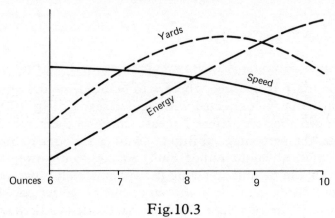

Fig.10.3

Arhythmic Golfers There appears to be a third type of golfer who is characterised perhaps by having a poor sense of rhythm and who could only swing easily with one club head weight as shown in Fig. 10.4. Either side of this critical weight, say, eight ounces, they slowed down their swings. I describe such golfers as arhythmic because they appear to be unable to adapt to the variety of different rhythms which different clubs demand.

In these tests I directly measured the swing speed on DOC and then calculated yardage based on the Golfing Society formula. Power in the club head was calculated in terms of its kinetic energy ($\frac{1}{2}mv^2$).

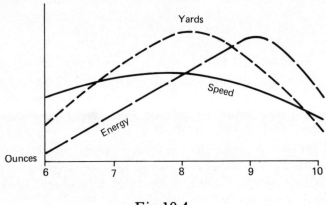

Fig.10.4

What does 'Type' imply?

This difference between three types of golfer, and there may be more than three, appears to be fundemental and not particularly connected with age or sex. In Fig. 10.5 are shown the ten golfers I measured as to their speed indices, the percentage ability to swing a six ounce club faster than an eight ounce club. At constant power a golfer should be able to swing the six ounce club twelve per cent faster than the eight ounce but no golfer could do this and the two Speed Golfers have speed indices of nine per cent. There was a bunch of seven Power Golfers whose Speed Indices were between nought and four per cent and with an average of two per cent. The one Arhythmic Golfer had a negative speed index of minus four-and-a-half per cent. But most significant from this chart of Fig. 10.5 is the clear gap between Power and Speed golfers.

At this stage I had no real idea of the cause of this difference and decided further measurements were required as in the next chapter.

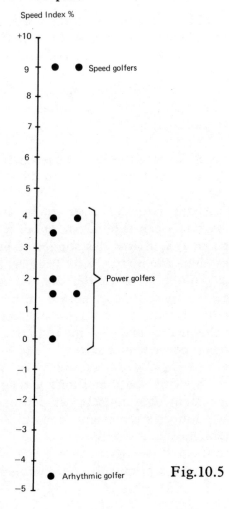

Fig.10.5

11

Further Reflections on Power and Speed Golfers

In this chapter I consider further the strange phenomenon revealed by the electronic robot DOC that there appear to be two main types of golfer and they can be easily distinguished by the relative degree with which they can swing a six ounce head club faster than an eight ounce head club. This differential I call the Speed Index and typically:

Speed Type Golfers   Speed Index about 1.09
Power Type Golfers   Speed Index about 1.02

This division is quite important because it means that Speed Golfers can take advantage of using lighter clubs as Dr David Williams has suggested but Power Golfers cannot and are better with heavier clubs. But since Power Golfers were in the distinct majority over my limited sample of ten golfers this must somewhat generally discount Dr Williams' theories. I have thought about this matter and give my tentative conclusions first and then proceed to elaborate:

1   High swing speed and long yardage is generated by the main body muscles as distinct from the hand-arm muscles representing about 80 per cent of our total muscular strength.

2   In the golf swing we can use effectively the whole of our hand-arm muscles (20 per cent of the total) but

we cannot use more than a fraction of our main body muscles (80 per cent of the total).

3   The reason why Power Golfers cannot swing appreciably faster with lighter clubs is that their main body muscle is 'slow muscle' and its slowness may well have a temperamental basis.

The muscular power for the golf swing

The energy which a professional golfer is able to develop in the club head at impact is about 200 foot pounds and we have to account for where this energy comes from as regards the golfer's muscles. The energy has to be developed over about .25 second and thus in the downswing the average rate of energy generation is $200/.25 = 800$ foot pounds per second or 1.45 horse-power.

An analysis of a typical male human being indicates about the following volumes of muscle:

Main body muscles from the shoulders down to the feet i.e. the twist or 'pivot' muscles	1200 cu. inches
The hand-arm muscles used in the arm-swinging of a golf club	250 cu. inches

Thus the main body muscles account for about 80 per cent of the total whilst the hand-arm muscles account for about 20 per cent of the total as referred to earlier.

Now if we take various human athletic activities it can be roughly calculated that the following energy expenditures are involved and assuming that all muscles can deliver the same energy per cubic inch then:

	Energy rate in Ft. pounds/sec.	Percentage total Muscular Capacity
Walking	200	13½
Running	400	27
Sprinting	900	60

From such figures we can assume that if *all* the muscles of the body were involved at maximum effort then an energy rate of 900/.6 = 1500 ft pounds per second would be available, some 2.7 horsepower. Thus we now have two important figures:

Maximum human power at the
athletic level   1500 ft pounds/sec.
Energy required for a pro golf swing
                                                                       800 ft pounds/sec.

Now assuming a professional golfer is an 'athlete' then the first conclusion is that he can only manage to get 800/1500 = 53 per cent of his peak muscular power into the club and that despite the fact that his effort is only required for .25 second, much shorter than the sprinter. One first wonders if the difference is accounted for by the fact that the golfer not only has to swing the club but he also has to swing himself. But having done the necessary calculations I assure my reader that the amount of energy in the golfer swinging himself is trifling compared with the energy going into the club head and thus the only conclusion we can draw, empirically, is:

> *Whilst the golfer appears to use all his main muscles for the golf shot, he cannot deliver the totality into the club. At best it would seem that the golfer can only deliver some 50 per cent of his muscle effort into ball yardage effort.*

The maximum muscular strength of golfers

I decided to find out something about the differing muscular power of golfers and for this I needed a strength tester.

Strength tester When it comes to an assessment of a person's overall strength it appears to be the common view that this relates to weight-lifting ability. The apparatus I constructed is shown in Fig. 11.1 (in the section of photographs) and consists of a double-ended bar on which to pull vertically in a weight-lifting fashion and the muscular force involved is transmitted via a hinged lever to a pair of bathroom scales whose dial reading can be noted. The apparatus has an advantage over a mere weight-lifting test in that the subject under test can make his pull in accordance with his reasonable judgment and my instructions that he must hold the pull for five seconds. I am glad to say we had no slipped discs as a result.

I tested six of my ten golfers (the rest were unavailable) on this device and the results were:

Golfer	1-Wood yardage	Golfer type	Pull strength in pounds
Mr A	246	Power	330
Mr B	240	Speed	330
Mr C	238	Power	300
Mr D	234	Power	154
Mr E	204	Power	140
Mrs F	185	Speed	70

These results are plotted in Fig. 11.2. I draw the following general conclusions:

1. Speed Golfers, as represented by Mr B, are not inferior to Power Golfers as represented by Mr A or Mr C, as regards their pull strength.
2. Muscular power as determined by pull strength has no proportional relation to golf yardage. For example, Mr D has only about half the pull strength of Mr A but can drive within ten yards or so of him.

The plot thickens!

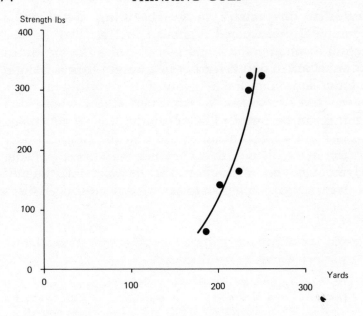

A piece of luck from an article in *The Times*

My analysis to date had indicated two things. In the first place it appeared that although all the main musculature of the body must be involved in the golf swing, yet only about 50 per cent of this found effectiveness in energy into the club head. In the second place, and somewhat sympathetic to such a conclusion, was the fact that maximum muscular power as determined by a weight-lifting sort of test had only a minor effect on golf yardage. It was while I was musing over the matter that I came across an article in *The Times* extracted from an earlier article in *Nature* on the subject of muscle *speeds* and I first give a summary:

The speed of muscle determined by nerve type

About twenty years ago Dr A. J. Buller and Dr John Eccles did an operation on the leg of a cat. The cat leg has both fast and slow muscles, the former being for the purpose of fast action and the latter for the slow adjustments of posture. They took the nerve from the fast muscle and transferred it to slow muscle and vice versa. The result was that the fast muscle became slow and the slow muscle became fast and this proved that muscle speed is related to the type of associated nerve. However, after a time the situation normalised itself and presumably this was due to the nerves becoming modified to agree with the proper functioning of the muscle.

The speed of muscle determined by electrical nerve pattern

Recently Dr S. Salmons of Birmingham University and Dr F. A. Sreter of Massachusetts have shown that it is the nature of the electrical pulses in the nerve fibre which determines muscle speed. They attached electronic stimulators to both fast and slow muscle nerves in cat muscle and showed that by artificially speeding up or slowing down the electrical nerve pattern they could control the speed of muscle response. Specifically they were able to make slow muscle fast and fast muscle slow. This suggests that since the animal psyche is on line to its own nervous system it can to some extent control its muscle speeds by modifying the nervous pattern to correspond to muscle utilisation intent. The animal gets the muscle speeds it needs in terms of its behavioural requirements.

What may be relevant in our search for the reasons differentiating Speed and Power Golfers is that:
1   There are fast and slow muscles in the human body.
2   Since the muscle speeds are under some degree of psychic control as to behavioural intent then:
The Speed Golfer may be one whose 'intent' is on swinging the club fast . . . a swinger.

The Power Golfer may be one whose 'intent' is to strike the ball a hard blow . . . a hitter.

Reaction time testing

I had previously reached the conclusions that the muscular strength of a golfer had little major effect on his club speed and yardage and also that the maximum power in the golf club was only about half that available in the golfer's muscles. But this latest evidence as to slow and fast muscle speeds suggested that both these phenomena might be due to the inability of the golfer to get his slow muscles effectively contributing to the golf swing. I wondered if this might be particularly true of the back muscles which are normally only used in a very slow fashion such as for balancing the body when sitting down.

But before attempting any further conclusions I decided to measure the reaction times of a few golfers. I did this because the cat experiments showed that muscle speed is related to nerve speeds and human reaction times are also related to nerve speeds..

Reaction time tester

I built a reaction time tester (Fig. 11.3 in the section of photographs) which consisted of a rotating cam and switches which illuminated one of three lamps in random order. All three lamps focussed into one photo-cell and when the latter was illuminated it permitted the escape of pulses at the rate of 250 per second into a counter. But if one put one's hand over the particular illuminated lamp then this stopped the escape of pulses. Thus the quicker one could move one's hand over the one of the three lamps which was illuminated, the lower the pulse count and the faster the reaction time. The lamps changed forty times over a two minute interval.

Fig. 8.1(a) Mr Keith Macdonald, Berkshire G.C. professional, driving through the first development model of DOC. For production model see Fig. 8.3

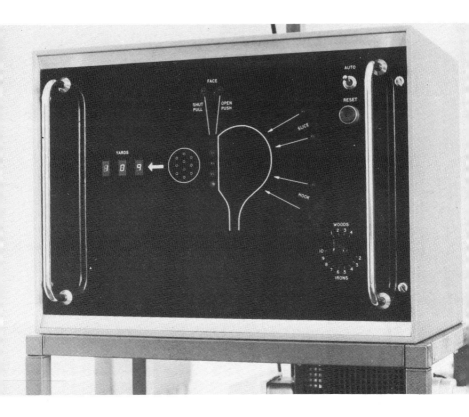

Fig. 8.1(b) The display panel of the original DOC shown in use in Fig. 8.1(a)

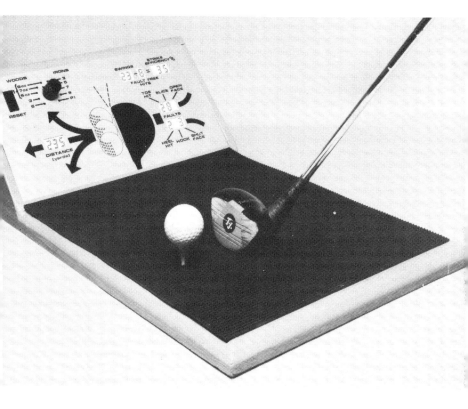

Fig. 8.3 The production model of DOC. The lamp (not shown) is an electric light bulb hung from the ceiling

Fig. 10.1 The author with the ten experimental 1-woods provided by the International Sports Company. The five in the left hand all have the same shafts but the head weights vary from 6 to 10 ounces in one-ounce increments. The group in the right hand all have a 7-ounce head weight but the shafts vary in whippiness from 4.6 to 3.5 cycles per second whip frequency

Fig. 11.1 The author's wife uses the strength tester

Fig. 11.3 Reaction time testing (Mr Andrew Reynolds, Assistant Professional Berkshire G.C. at the time of the tests. He is now professional at Deal G.C.)

Fig. 12.1 *Top*
Body-Twist and
Bottom
Shoulder-Arm
Rock (Mr Andy
Hall, Assistant
Professional, Berk-
shire Golf Club)

Fig. 14.1 The author and shaft whippiness tester

I carried out tests on four golfers about whom I had considerable measured information from DOC and especially as to their Speed Indices (the ability to swing a six ounce head faster than an eight ounce head). The results are as follows and as plotted in Fig. 11.4:

Golfer type	Speed index	Reaction time
Speed	1.09	.26 second
Power	1.04	.31 second
Power	1.02	.35 second
Power	1.01	.38 second

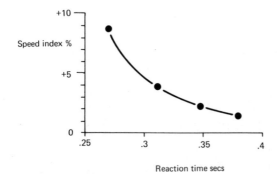

Fig.11.4

I confess I do not like experiments of this nature involving only four golfers but the values obtained fitted on such a smooth curve that I had to accept them as significant, with the main (tentative) conclusion that a Speed Golfer is a person with a fast reaction time and also that it seemed that Power Golfers varied among themselves in that those with the slower reaction times were least able to swing lighter clubs faster.

In general these findings tended to support the earlier conclusions in this chapter that a Speed Golfer is one whose psychic intent is on speed rather than force and has a fast reaction time, while a Power Golfer's sense of intent is associated with 'hitting the ball' more by force than swing speed. I began to come to the view that certain people had a 'speed feel' whilst others had more of a 'force feel' and in athletics the extreme examples of the two types would be a sprinter compared with a weight-lifter. There was certainly a bonus in the matter for the Speed Golfer since he could drive as far as the Power Golfer with only 80 per cent of the effort using lighter and faster clubs.

Thus the Speed Golfer was more efficient than a Power Golfer and this fact we now explore further.

12

Golf Swing Efficiency

It seems clear that in golf there are two main requirements for efficiency which when combined give the
golfer's overall stroke efficiency. This can be stated as an
equation:

Golfer's Stroke Efficiency = Swing Efficiency ×
Strike Efficiency

Where: Swing Efficiency is the ability to generate
club head speed for the minimum muscular effort.

Strike Efficiency is the ability to realise the first
three Impact Imperatives related to club squareness,
ball centrality and strike direction.

In this chapter we shall consider the first of the two
requirements as to Swing Efficiency which relates to
that Fourth Impact Imperative to get adquate club head
speed and power at impact. At the end of the last chapter
I noted that the Speed Golfer could get about the same
yardage for considerably less muscle effort than the
Power Golfer but I now go into this in some detail.
Fortunately the two assistant professionals at the Berkshire Golf Club were an ideal contrasting pair and the
following table gives their comparative performance and
characteristics. I refer to Mr Andy Hall as 'Mr Speed'
and to Mr Andrew Reynolds as 'Mr Power'.

Aspect	Mr Speed	Mr Power
Handicap	Scratch	Scratch
Standard Drive Yardage	240	246
Swing speed ft/second	162	155
Preferred club head weight	6 ounces	8½ ounces
Club impact energy in foot pounds	200	251
Weight lifting strength in pounds	330	330
Reaction time in seconds	.26	.31
Energy per yard in foot pounds	.835	1.02
Relative energy efficiency	100 per cent	82 per cent

In considering relative energy efficiency I have given Mr Speed a nominal value of 100 per cent to establish a datum. Thus we find that two golfers of just about the same golfing ability at scratch handicap have an 18 per cent difference in their Swing Efficiency, because Mr Speed can swing a light club appreciably faster than Mr Power. His reduced yardage of six yards is probably of negligible golfing significance.

Comparing two Typical Golfers

But being professionals Mr Speed and Mr Power are not Typical Golfers and so we next compare two Typical Golfers who have very similar golfing ability. The first I shall call Mrs Speed and the second I call Dr Power (myself). The significant figures are:

Aspect	Mrs Speed	Dr Power
Standard drive yardage	200	200
Club impact energy foot pounds.	127	139
Club head weight	6 ounces	8 ounces
Relative swing efficiency	100 per cent	91 per cent

If I (Dr Power) could swing at Mrs Speed's efficiency I could add about ten yards to my drive but I simply cannot swing a light club fast enough even though it takes no more total muscular power.

I experiment on my swing speed—the two factors in the swing

I confess I would like to add ten yards to my drive for no extra total effort. I spent days with electronic DOC measuring my swing speed with all sorts of swing styles and all sorts of clubs but with no appreciable difference from my standard swing speed of about 125 feet per second. But as a result of thinking about the matter and pondering on the facts about slow and fast muscles I came to some conclusions which are based upon the apparent fact that the swing involves two distinct muscular zones of the body:

1 *Body-Twist* This takes place essentially in a horizontal plane (the 'pivot') and consists roughly of a 45 degree rotation of the hips plus a further 45 degree rotation of the shoulders so that the total rotation of the shoulders is about 90 degrees relative to the feet. One presumes that this is the main source of swing power since it could involve about 80 per cent of the body muscles.

2 *Shoulder-Arm Rock* This takes place essentially in a vertical plane and consists partly of a rocking motion of the shoulders (left shoulder down and right shoulder up) plus an extra further rock of the arms.

It is the combination of these two features, one in a horizontal plane and one in a vertical plane, which gives a result in an inclined plane. These two aspects are shown in Fig. 12.1 (in the section of photographs) and were posed by Mr Speed (Mr Andy Hall). They are not the complete swing since the Shoulder-Arm Rock goes finally into a bending of the right elbow and a wrist hinge-cock. But what these photos show is the two main aspects of the *power house* of the swing. One source of power is a horizontal Body-Twist and the other source of power is a vertical Shoulder-Arm Rock.

I then did tests on myself to see how fast I could execute these two movements taken separately. The times given relate to one quarter of a complete cycle of centre-right-centre-left-centre and I did about ten such swings continuously and timed the totality. Thus the deduced quarter cycle time should represent my downswing time. The results were:

Body-Twist time	.32 second
Shoulder-Arm Rock time	.25 second
Known actual downswing time	.32 second

Now this result is very interesting since it is clear that for a synchronised swing the Body-Twist time and the Shoulder-Arm Rock time should be the same. But in my case it appeared equally clear that I had a time bottleneck in the system which was my slow Body-Twist time at .32 second. Furthermore this result also showed a known problem in my personal golf which is the danger of my arms trying to come through in .25 second and leaving my body behind at .32 second downswing times. Thus I am in danger of a non-synchronised two-piece swing in which my arm effort and body effort are not synchronised at impact.

I then asked Mr Speed to repeat my experiments but his Body-Twist and his Shoulder-Arm Rock were *identical for downswing time*. This suggested that a Speed Golfer is one who can swing both his power sources in synchronism and not only achieve a one-piece swing but also make demands on that one-piece swing to speed it up without running into a bottleneck from his Body-Twist.

The specification of a Speed Golfer

It was becoming increasingly clear as to the nature of Speed Golfers who have a much higher swing efficiency than Power Golfers and I think the full specification is:

A Speed Golfer is one with *faster main body muscles* than a Power Golfer i.e. he has a faster 'pivot' which can keep up with his Shoulder-Arm Rock.

I also conclude that if anyone wished to increase his golf yardage the only hope would be to speed up his pivot or body twist. Perhaps this is the reason why professionals advocate 'getting the left hip out of the way' at the start of the downswing i.e. what they are really after is a fast Body-Twist. Incidentally this reminded me of the tests I had done on DOC (Chapter 9) with Mr Neil Coles who had an extremely fast downswing Body-Twist and who struck the ball at 180 feet a second, an extremely high speed. I would take a bet that Mr Coles is a Speed Golfer.

How fast can a Speed Golfer swing?

Although I have just reported that Mr Speed (Andy Hall) swings at 162 feet a second I wondered if this was his maximum swing speed or merely the one he found convenient and which lets him play within himself. I thus had a special session on DOC with Mr Speed in which he went all out for maximum swing speed with a six ounce club. The results are given in Fig. 12.2 and we first checked Mr Speed's Speed Index using all the five 1-Woods from six to ten ounce head weights in one ounce increments and this showed that he had hardly changed at all over the six months since he had been previously measured. It confirmed him as a Speed Golfer with a normal maximum swing speed of just over 160 feet a second with a six ounce club. He then went all out for a swing speed record and secured a swing speed of 185 feet per second which would have corresponded to a drive yardage of 274 yards and with a downswing time of about .21 second. This is shown at 'challenge' on Fig. 12.2.

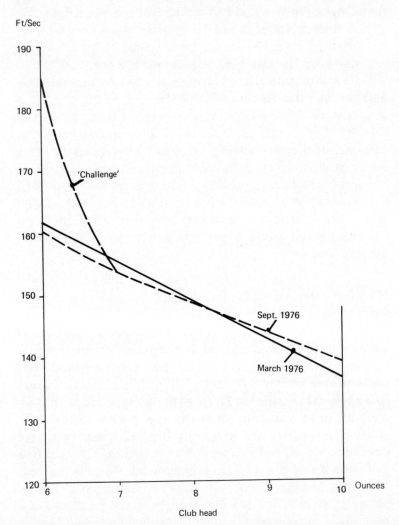

Ft/Sec

'Challenge'

Sept. 1976

March 1976

Ounces

Club head

Conclusions on Speed and Power Golfers

My conclusions are as follows:
1   The Speed Golfer is one whose Body-Twist and
     Shoulder-Arm Rock can be powered at the same

maximum speed and thus they lock-in together in a single integrated one-piece rhythm. Thus they can force this system to very high swing speeds without danger of 'coming apart'.

2   The Power Golfer is one whose Body-Twist speed is naturally slower than (more 'slow muscle'?) his Shoulder-Arm Rock and if he is to swing reliably then this must be tuned to his slower Body-Twist. Possibly this is the basis for the general tendency towards slower backswings to slow down the pace of the Shoulder-Arm Rock to come into line with the Body-Twist. There is great danger of the Power Golfer 'coming apart' if he allows his arms to dominate in the swing.

A little point for later consideration – the importance of the *common* shoulder in two swing motions

The analysis I have given of dividing the main swing action in the two aspects of Body-Twist and Shoulder-Arm Rock pinpoints a matter which could be of great importance which I shall deal with in a later chapter. This is due to the fact that only the shoulders are equally represented in both the Body-Twist or pivot and in the Shoulder-Arm Rock. The shoulder motion is the end point and objective of the Body-Twist and it is also the starting feature of the Shoulder-Arm Rock.

The shoulders are thus *common* to both features of the swing. This implies that if we take the view that a one-piece swing is desirable in which there is synchronous integration of both Body-Twist and Shoulder-Arm Rock then *the common centre of harmonisation must be in the shoulders*. Put in another fashion, the sense of conscious rhythm in the golfer's swing must be centred in his shoulder motion.

Later we shall see that there is a second and quite

distinct reason why this should be so when we analyse the swing flail action and the shoulders as the 'hand' which operates the flail. We shall thus see that since the golfer only has a limited amount of free consciousness at the disposal of his attention during the swing this must be focussed in the shoulders. But now I get ahead of myself!

13

Golf Strike Efficiency and Postural Wander

In the last chapter I suggested the formula:

Golf-stroke Efficiency = Swing Efficiency
× Strike Efficiency

I have dealt a little with Swing Efficiency, so next let us turn to Strike Efficiency which relates to how accurately the club struck the ball as to the first Three Impact Imperatives of squareness, centrality and direction.

In this chapter I shall only consider the implications of the Third Law of Cussedness on the situation and the fact, which I have also described as 'Jelly-on-Springs', that the human being has considerable postural wander. Furthermore I shall only deal with one main aspect of Strike Efficiency and that is the need to hit the ball with the centre of the club. The permissible wander from this position is only about ⅜ inch, as we considered in chapter 3. Now this is a remarkable requirement for accuracy and especially as we shall see that Jelly-on-Springs can have postural wander of several inches and in several directions.

In order to evaluate the problem I carried out a number of very simple experiments which my reader could easily repeat for himself. This I recommend because I am fast coming to the conclusion that in considering Golf-Stroke Efficiency it is Strike Efficiency which is far more important and vulnerable than Swing Efficiency. Many people have quite adequate swings but are all over the course due to low and unreliable Strike Efficiency.

Posture

The ability of the body to take up many postural modes is not due to a given (skeleton) bone since bones are rigid and fixed but it is the *joints* which permit a pair of bones to have a hinging or rotating relationship to each other. Some of these joints are simple hinges (such as the knee) whilst some are two-direction hinges (such as the wrist). Other joints are even more complex (such as the hip joint) and combine a two-directional hinge with rotational motion, a sort of universal joint.

Slack-Motion and End-Stops

If one examines the motion of the human joints one finds that:

1   There is a zone of easy motion which is the characteristic motion of the joint and this I call Slack-Motion.

2   At each extreme end of the Slack-Motion it comes up against End-Stops.

As applied to some of the significant golfing joints, and the possibility of Jelly-on-Springs faults, typical figures are:

Joint	*Slack-Motion*
Ankles (rolling mode)	40 degrees
Ankles (up-down foot mode)	60 degrees
Knees (bending mode)	120 degrees
Knees (sideways bending mode)	nil
Hips (sidesway mode)	14 inches
Hips (forward sway)	4 inches
Hips (rotation of pair)	90 degrees
Wrists (holding club):	
Hinging mode	90 degrees
Cocking mode	90 degrees
Rolling mode	90 degrees
Shoulders (rotation relative to hips)	90 degrees

The above appear to be the main Slack-Motions relevant to the golfer.

Slack-Motions relevant to club-ball alignment

There are three principal Slack-Motions which are relevant as to how accurately the club face is centrally aligned to the ball at impact. They are Sidesway, Forward-Sway and Bounce (see Fig. 13.3).

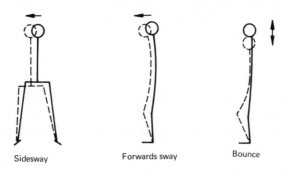

Sidesway   Forwards sway   Bounce

Fig.13.3

Sidesway
If one sways sideways during the backswing and does not sidesway to an equal and opposite extent on the downswing, then it is clear that the club will impact the ball in a different position from the alignment at the address. In general it will create a club arc biassed behind the ball and the golfer will hit the ground before the ball.
Experiment With the feet about 22 inches apart, put the right arm forwards to line up with a mark on the wall. Sway right and left from centre and note the distance the hand moves along the wall relative to the mark. It will be found that this will be something like seven inches either side of centre as the main weight comes onto the right and then the left foot.

Such a degree of Slack-Motion is potentially disastrous for the golfer since his natural chance of an equal counter-sway in the downswing is very uncertain. The only answer to this problem is to curtail sidesway severely by methods to be considered in a later chapter.

Forwards Sway

If one has correctly aligned the club to the ball at the address, then any Forward Sway towards the ball during the swing will tend to cause one to hit the ball with the heel and any backwards sway will tend to cause one to hit the ball with the toe. Note that both such sways are across the strike line.

Experiment

Hold a club in the address position and take a stance with the body balance well back on the heels and note the ground position of the toe of the club. In this posture it can be shown (by means of bathroom scales and a thick book) that about 90 per cent of the body weight is supported by the heels and about 10 per cent is on the balls of the feet.

Next allow the body weight to move forwards (towards the ball) until the weight is about equally distributed between heel and ball of each foot. Observe the new position of the club head toe and it will be found that it has moved forwards about four inches towards the ball.

Now we know from that Second Impact Imperative that the club should strike the ball within ⅜ inch of centrality but how can it do this if there is a four inch Slack-Motion simply due to the way in which our weight is balanced on our feet? This we shall consider later.

Bounce

If we bounce up and down during the swing, then we shall top the ball if we are bouncing upwards, and we shall hit the ground behind the ball and lose speed and yardage if we are bouncing downwards.

Experiment. Stand with the knees right back so that the legs are straight and hold an arm forwards to a mark on the wall. Then bend the knees progressively so that one's height is shortened, and measured by the lowering of the arm pointing towards the wall. If one checks the mathematics of the geometry the following table tells us the correlation between knee-bending and 'bounce' height shortening:

Angle of legs from vertical	Forwards motion of knees	Drop in height
0	0	0
5 degrees	1.57 inches	.14 inches
10 degrees	2.72 inches	.6 inches
15 degrees	4.66 inches	1.26 inches

Now if our height is bobbing up and down, the golf club head will be doing the same relative to the ground. The above table tells us that a forwards kneecrack of 2.72 inches is changing our height to the ball by .6 inch which is dangerously over the permissible wander limit of ⅜ inch (.375 inch) permitted by that Second Impact Imperative concerned with central alignment of club and ball. To be on the safe side we would do better to crack our knees forwards only by 5 degrees (1.57 inches) and thus suffer a negligible change of height of .14 inch. This will be reconsidered later but it suggests that we are advised 'to stand up' somewhat in our stance to minimise bouncing.

The conscious use of End-Stops to reduce Slack-Motion

The characteristic curve of a human joint is shown in Fig. 13.2 There is a central zone of Slack-Motion of high positional indeterminancy and it is this which is responsible for swaying and bouncing. The motion is so easy that it is difficult to be sure 'where one is'. The centre of this Slack-Motion is the point of maximum relaxation and it is the position which the joint will naturally take up if it has no work to do. But this also warns us that to take a stance or swing a club in the most relaxed fashion will place us at the very centre of the Slack-Motions and with the maximum likelihood of easy postural wander such as swaying and bouncing. Thus 'relaxation' is not such a golfing virtue as some would have us believe.

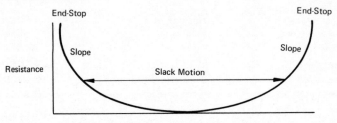

Fig. 13.2

But the positions where postural form is fixed are the End-Stops and there is also high resistance to change of posture in motion which relates to the approach slopes to the End-Stops and which I shall call the Stop-Slopes. It is true that such Stop-Slopes are both uphill and downhill according to the direction of motion and it is only the Uphill-Stop-Slope which is stable i.e. a form of body motion in which one is moving towards an End-Stop. This gives us one key as to how to reduce swaying and bouncing which we consider in a later chapter.

Counter End-Stops

Fortunately human limbs are constructed in pairs and each unit of the pair is a mirror image of the other. This means that the End-Stops in a pair of limbs can act against each other and this effect I call Counter End-Stops. It is illustrated in Fig. 13.3. By suitably positioning the two limbs of a pair (for example by clasping the hands together) it is found the slack motion of one limb can be reduced by the Uphill-Stop-Slope of the other limb and vice versa.

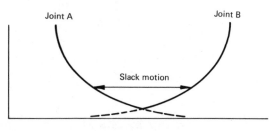

Fig. 13.3

Experiment. Hold the right hand straight out and rotate it. It will be found that it can rotate about 180 degrees between its End-Stops. Now repeat the experiment with the left hand and we find the same result.

Now put the palms of the hands together and it will be found that the rotation between joint End-Stops has been reduced to 90 degrees from 180 degrees. Furthermore if (thumbs uppermost) one rotates clockwise it will be found that it is the right hand End-Stop which stops the rotation when the left hand could have gone on for a further 90 degrees or more and with the opposite effect on anti-clockwise rotation.

Second experiment – Sidesway reduction by Counter End-Stops. Take a golfing stance with the feet some 22 inches apart and note how easy it is to sidesway. Next put the weight on the insteps of the feet by rolling the feet towards each other so that each comes up against its inwards-rolling End-Stops. This position almost elimi-nates sidesway (in a later chapter I refer to it as the Ski Stance) since sway to the right is inhibited by the foot rolling End-Stop of the left foot and vice versa.

Later in this book, in dealing with how to control those five Laws of Cussedness, I make some use of technique based on the properties of End-Stop-Slopes and of Counter End-Stops.

14
Club Whip Mythology

I had thoroughly investigated the effect of using clubs with differing head weights as described in Chapter 10 and this had revealed the two main types of golfer as to Speed and Power. In further analysing the matter in Chapters 11 and 12 I concluded that a Power Golfer was one whose Body-Twist is slower than his Shoulder-Arm Rock and that it was desirable that such golfers should let their swing timing agree with the slower function, the Body-Twist. In turn this suggested that Power Golfers, the major group, should have a slow backswing in harmony with their slow Body-Twist and all my experience since coming to that conclusion has strengthened it.

But I next wished to explore an entirely different aspect of the swing and that related to the use of stiff or whippy clubs. The question of club whip is one of the central fascinating features of golf mythology and I have never met a golfer, amateur or professional, who did not consider that club whip mattered. I think this centres on the fact that we all can feel when a club is 'right' for us and I later found that head weight was not the prime variable in the question of 'feel' but it was shaft whip.

When a golf club 'feels right' it is due to shaft whippiness

The International Sports Company very kindly made up

for me five 1-Woods all of the same 7-ounce head weight and shaft length but with different whippinesses of shaft extending from 4.6 cycles per second as the stiffest and 3.5 cycles per second as the most whippy. Now I loaned these clubs to various golfers and asked them to tell me if they had a marked preference for one club or the other and in every case they were able to make an unambiguous choice in terms of 'feeling right' and getting a good result on the course. The selection of the preferred club differed widely so that it was a Jack Sprat situation, but when I analysed the preferences in terms of the golfers' known driving characteristics and swing speed I found that there was an exact correlation in that:

The preferred club was the one whose whip cycle time was the same as the golfer's downswing time

The total correlating table was:

Club	Club whip frequency cycles/sec.	Club whip time and golfer's downswing time in seconds	Golfer's Impact Speed in ft/sec.	1-Wood yardage
A	4.6	.22	160	260
B	4.4	.23	150	245
C	4.1	.24	145	235
D	3.8	.26	135	220
E	3.5	.28	125	200

The correlation between Impact Speed and Downswing Time can be given approximately if one assumes that all golfers have about the same length of swing arc (such as 17.5 feet). In that case we have the simple formula:

$$\frac{VT}{2} = 17.5$$

and $VT = 35$ (= 'K' below)

where:
V is Impact Speed in feet/second

T is downswing time in seconds

The constant 'K' appears to be quite close to 35 as independently assessed by the preference of a golfer of known Impact Speed for a club of known whippiness. This means that one can choose a club of preferred whippiness from either of the two formulae:

Shaft whip frequency = Impact speed / 35
or Shaft whip frequency = Standard Yardage / 57

In the latter case Impact Speed is converted to Standard Yardage through the intermediate constant 1.62 which is widely used to correlate Impact Speed and Yardage.

Now most golfers do not know what their Impact Speed is since they do not have access to the required electronic measuring apparatus but they do have a good idea of their yardage (1-Wood) under average conditions. In which case they can use the second formula (Shaft whip frequency = Yardage / 57) to find what would be a whippy club frequency which would suit them. Accordingly the following table holds for different types of golfer:

Type of golfer	Yardage	Desirable whip frequency
Top pro	285	5.0
Average pro } Top amateur	240	4.2
Male week-end golfer under 45	230	4.0
As above – lady	205	3.6
Male week-end golfer over 50	210	3.7
As above – lady	185	3.3
Male senior citizen (over 65)	195	3.4
As above – lady	170	3.0

I myself am age 68 and my standard drive is about 200 yards. I need a club whip frequency of 3.5 cycles. I have such a club and find it the best driver I have ever possessed.

Measuring whip frequency

In order to get my facts right about the whippiness of different clubs I constructed the apparatus shown in Fig. 14.1 (in the section of photographs). This consists of clamping the club grip in a bench vice and arranging a lamp and photocell so that the latter was darkened if the club whipped in front of it. In turn the photocell gave out an electronic impulse which was fed to an electromagnet adjacent to the shaft so that the shaft whip was sustained in its vibrations automatically. By taking the photocell impulses to an electronic counter and timing this over (say) 100 seconds, the whip frequency can be determined with great accuracy.

An experiment on DOC

I next did a personal experiment on DOC with the two extreme clubs in my range of five, all of which had the same weight and shaft lengths, and the results were:

Club whip frequency	Impact Speed	Yardage
4.6 cycles	123 ft/sec	200
3.5 cycles	133 ft/sec	216

This indicated that a club which was tuned to myself at 3.5 cycles increased my swing speed by an amount which corresponded to an extra 16 yards in 200 yards, a most handsome gain.

A dilemma

In his book *The Science of The Golf Swing*, Dr David

Williams states that club whippiness can do nothing for one and at most one could conceive a margin of five yards in 200 yards due to 'whipping through', although he makes the case that one cannot meet the various conditions for this to be possible. Now I had shown a factual increase of club speed equal to 16 yards in 200 yards and yet I had to accept Dr Williams' analysis that club whip as such (in terms of pure mechanics) can do almost nothing for club speed.

But I recalled my work with Speed and Power Golfers and decided that the result I was getting was of a similar nature in that if a club 'feels right' then one can swing it faster and get more yardage. Thus it appeared that the analysis was primarily psychological but the improved psychology gave better mechanical results. I find this the only possible explanation in view of Dr Williams' rigorous proof that whippiness mechanics cannot add yardage. But apparently whippiness psychology can! The problem and phenomena belonged to the realm of Psycho-Golf.

Club whippiness and Psycho-Golf

I take stock:

1   In terms of pure mechanics club whip cannot increase club head speed at impact.
2   A golfer can swing a club which 'feels right' faster than a club which 'feels wrong'.
3   It appears that a club 'feels right' when its whip frequency period (the time for one cycle of whip) is the same as the downswing time.

Now I think I have elucidated the reconciliation of all the above three factors but since this involves some trigonometrical analysis I have relegated the full explanation to Appendix 1 ('Club Whip and the Flail Swing') but here I will state the main conclusions involved:

a) the golf downswing involves a certain *critical timing* which is of the same nature as the critical timing in:

  (i)   cracking a whip
  (ii) casting a fly-fisherman's rod
  (iii) throwing a cricket ball
  (iv) serving a tennis ball

In each of the above cases we are in the realms of flail mechanics in which 'a first swinging lever drives a second swinging lever'. This has sometimes been called the double pendulum effect.

b) In such cases there is a basically slow motion and then 'something whips through' and thus the golf downswing is fundamentally asymmetrical.

c) Nevertheless such asymmetry of effort and motion has its own asymmetrical 'feel' as to timing and rhythm.

d) A corresponding asymmetry of timing 'feel' is provided by a golf club whose whip cycle time is the same as the downswing time because during the downswing the whip changes direction in that it first opposes the downswing by bending backwards and then supports the downswing by bending forwards. Thus the whip changes its mechanical impedance from opposition to assistance to provide the exact timing asymmetry which is characteristic of the flail nature of the swing i.e. the *shaft whip is in synchronisation with the flail swing*.

e) Overall, the feel of the shaft whip gives the golfer the correct clue as to desirable downswing timing and acts like an orchestrating metronome for the swing timing.

I leave the matter at that point since we are now getting into the depths of Psycho-Golf, but for those with a scientific turn of mind the analysis is given more fully in Appendix 1.

But you cannot buy such clubs!

Earlier in this chapter I have given a classified list of
eight sorts of golfer and their ideal club whip fre-
quencies. But not all the classifications can buy correct
clubs since the whippiest normal club ('ladies whippy')
still has a stiffness corresponding to a whip frequency of
about 4.1 cycles. This means that the majority of Typical
Golfers (and especially older Typical Golfers) cannot
buy clubs which suit them as to more whippiness and
they certainly cannot buy clubs whose whippiness is
ideally 'tuned' to their swing speeds.

That is a pity but perhaps publishing this book may
stimulate a little study and action by the club-makers.

The main characteristic whereby existing golf clubs are
classified for sale is the so-called Swing Weight, which is
concerned only with the head weight and takes no account
of shaft stiffness or whippiness. I have thoroughly analysed
the Swing Weight approach and it is simply nonsense. The
same remarks apply to the Matched Clubs mythology as
possibly an even bigger nonsense.

The prime basis for club classification and matching
must be a combination of head weight and whippiness to
suit the known swing speed of the individual golfer. Golf
clubs should be 'tailored' to suit the individual like a
well-fitting suit of clothes. We now have the science to do
it.

15
Other Experiments on Golf Clubs

All my experiments on golf clubs have been with the 1-Wood (driver) and I limited myself to this single club as soon as I began to realise what a great deal was to be learned about its use, certainly enough to fill a book. Thus far my experiments have been as to:

Head weights

Over the six to ten ounce head weights:

Speed Golfers are most natural with, and get best yardage from, a six ounce head. Incidentally this is about the weight of a head without any lead in it.

Power Golfers are most natural with, and get best yardage from, a club in the seven and a half to eight and a half ounce head weight. There is little to choose between these head weights but since it is desirable to have a bias to help against fatigue I would choose a seven and a half ounce head weight.

Whippiness

Here we are in the realms of Psycho-Golf and the confidence which 'right feel' brings, possibly related to synchronisation of timing when the shaft whip is tuned to the downswing time. Unfortunately such clubs cannot be bought at the present time although I have explored the practicability of making whippy clubs with steel shafts and this is quite easy providing one reduces the diameter (at the grip end) from ½ inch to $7/16$ inch.

But I also explored other aspects of clubs and give the results for the record.

Over-damped clubs

Since I had explored golf club whippiness I decided to experiment with clubs without any whip at all. It was quite difficult to make these and I experimented with filling the shafts with various viscous mastics. The final answer was to take about a two foot length of steel shaft coated with a damping mastic (such as Seelastic) and to ram this down inside the club shaft until the mastic was about $1/32$ inch thick. One thus had an excellent damping effect as the two shafts 'fought' each other through the layer of mastic. The psychological effect of handling such a club was considerable. If you let the head of a normal club drop onto a hard surface it will bounce in a lively manner but the damped club fell with a sickening thud.

In playing with such a club on the course, or swinging it for speed measurement through DOC, there was no appreciable difference.

Shaft materials

I experimented with carbon fibre shafts and with titanium shafts which take two and one ounces respectively off the shaft weights. In playing with such clubs on the course or swinging through DOC there was no appreciable difference.

Floating lead clubs

It is well known that a club only imparts about half its energy into the ball because there is an 'impedance mismatch' due to the club head being stiffer and heavier than the ball. I experimented on reducing the mechanical impedance of a club by removing all the lead from a 1-Wood and then I put back two ounces of lead so that it 'floated' behind the club-face and up against a rubber cushion. The idea was for the lead weight to make its impact on the ball in a slower and more progressive fashion. The impact should have been 'softer'.

In playing on the course or swinging through DOC there was no appreciable difference.

The club-makers have it nearly right

Apart from the Speed Golfer, who should choose lighter head weights, the club-makers have it nearly right on club design characteristics. Indeed they have it almost exactly right in the design of clubs for professionals and top grade amateurs and I refer particularly to whippiness characteristics.

All the club-makers (as far as I know) use professionals to make final judgments on new clubs and professionals are quite right in approving existing designs *for themselves*. Modern clubs *are* right for professionals.

But they are *not* right for Typical Golfers and no club-maker (again, as far as I know) has set out to find the desirable characteristics of Typical Golfer clubs, especially as regards whippiness.

And yet 90 per cent of the club market is for Typical Golfers and I suspect that a good new market awaits the club-maker who will design clubs for the Typical Golfer which have 'tuned whippiness'.

16

Reflections on the New Experimental Data

In Part 1 on Preliminary Thoughts I recorded some definite ideas as to those Four Impact Imperatives and those Five Laws of Cussedness which impeded their actualisation. But by the end of Part 1 my positive ideas were so covered by the smokescreen of golf mythology including both wild and prejudiced opinions (and I include my own) that I finally had to decide: 'Get thee to a laboratory!'

Part 2 describes what I found in the laboratory and a year and several thousand pounds later I take stock of what I found.

I have to confess that my investigations were somewhat patchy. Sometimes, as in exploring the effect of club head weights I had conducted the tests in a systematic fashion so that the conclusions I came to had a reasonable degree of statistical validity. At other times, as in the work on shaft whippiness, I had mainly used myself as guinea pig apart from asking other golfers which club felt right. Sometimes I had used about five golfers to secure indications and such applied to the measurements on muscular strength and reaction times.

Nevertheless I achieved my main objective of securing some new measured data on golfers and I summarise my findings as follows:

The main problem of Typical Golfers is inconsistency

Altogether I have conducted measurements on about 120

Typical Golfers as to swing speeds and impact faults (on DOC) and these showed conclusively that the main problem for Typical Golfers is inconsistency of accurate impact with the ball. Most golfers are reasonably consistent with their swing speeds and what I have called Swing Efficiency, but their problem is Strike Efficiency and the first three of those Four Impact Imperatives as to squareness, centrality and club direction.

I consider that such a finding justifies what I stated in Chapter 2, that golf is a 'systems problem' and is not a problem of any single golfing feature and I deduce that there is no single 'secret of golf'. I have analysed the Typical Golfer as having a Proper Par Handicap of nine (actual average handicap of 13) and this proves that the Typical Golfer plays perfect golf on half the holes but drops a stroke on each of the other half. Furthermore this inconsistency is not systematic but is statistical and the Typical Golfer never knows when he is going to play a hole well or badly.

Thus the difference between the Good Golfer and the Typical Golfer is a difference of consistency and I suspect (from mentally reviewing my friends of both sorts) that this is not related to the relative amount of practice but is due to the different degree of *mental grip* which they have on the game. This is illustrated also by how the Typical Golfer can run into a 'bad patch' and be slicing, hooking and topping with successive strokes. This can only be due to having made one bad shot which he then tries to correct from inadequate mental resource. The Good Golfer is one who can put himself right immediately because he understands the causality of the game, i.e. what acts cause what results.

I now come to a first major conclusion:

The problems of the Typical Golfer are in the psyche. He lacks an accurate model of 'Golf Causality'

Golf may be a game played with the muscles, but it is kept on beam with the head.

Golfing types

I think the division of golfing types into Speed and Power is important and particularly the explanation I derive that the Speed Golfer is one whose Body-Twist and Shoulder-Arm Rock are synchronised naturally at the same speed. By contrast the Power Golfer is one who cannot move his body as fast as his arms and is thus in danger of a two-piece asynchronous swing. Such golfers must slow up their swing to suit their Body-Twist and probably this is why they do better with heavier clubs, which also tend to slow things down.

The majority of golfers have a fixed, unalterable swing speed

Another finding of significance is that the majority of golfers can do little to speed up their swings for longer yardage. The DOC results confirmed what we are so used to witnessing on the golf course, that when a golfer tries to swing 'flat out' the ball goes no further and is likely to go astray due to lower Strike Efficiency. Such results relate to the weight-lifting tests which showed how little total muscular power comes into ball yardage, probably because we cannot power our 'slow muscle' into the ball sufficiently to be of any appreciable use.

The ignorance of golfers as to swing speed and yardage

Another quaint fact was that I never found a Typical Golfer who had any idea of his own swing speed or his yardage on the course. I found this most odd since golf is such a yardage game. In order to know one's yardage all one need know is how many walking paces go to a hundred yards (in my case 115) and thus any shot can be paced. Furthermore I noted that Typical Golfers had no accurate idea of distances and mainly selected the club to use by instinct. This is all very well in its way but can lead to serious misjudgments. This may be why the American professionals are better than the British in that the Americans are much more numerically minded. They seem to know exactly how far each club will carry under standard conditions and what allowances then to make for terrain and weather so that they can choose the correct club with a forecast length accuracy of about five yards.

This sort of ignorance by the Typical Golfer is a further example of lack of *mental grip* on the game.

All players could play to single figures if they were accurate

If we consider a golfer of (say) 70 years of age who can drive 195 yards and have a fairway shot of 160 yards then such a golfer, assuming 2 putts per green, can:

Score Par on 3-Pars up to 195 yards
Score Par on 4-Pars up to 355 yards
Score Par on 5-Pars up to 515 yards

A study of our two courses at the Berkshire Club shows that such a performance would only drop five shots in the round and thus a person of any age (and certainly into the 70s) can play to single figures providing he can play his shots consistently and providing he can judge accurately as to direction and distance.

The strange case of 'Frank'

In our Artisans section at the Berkshire ("The Forest

Artisans') we have a unique character known as 'Frank'. I recently played in a match against Frank, who is 79 years old, and noted:

a)   Frank has a handicap of eight which means he has to play 'to his age' to be round in his handicap

b)   The match was a foursome but it was clear that Frank was playing to a handicap of about four and this was due to astonishing accuracy

c)   Frank was not a long driver, about 190 yards

Now I had never before played with anyone who could 'play to his age' and certainly not to four strokes better than his age but it was clear from talking with Frank that this (unique?) feat was quite normal for him.

Frank proved the point I am making that anyone can play to single figures based on *accuracy* of judgment and performance. It convinced me that what matters in golf is not Swing Efficiency but Strike Efficiency related to the first three of those Four Impact Imperatives. I suspect one can get by with any old swing providing the Strike Efficiency is high.

Club whippiness

The most important factor in the selection of golf clubs is that they should 'feel right'. The first factor involved is the club head weight and we have seen how Speed Golfers should have lighter clubs (also vide Dr David Williams) but that Power Golfers are better with heavier clubs. The second aspect of 'feeling right' is that the clubs should have an appropriate whippiness. I have suggested that this should be tailored to the individual golfer and that the whip period should be the same as his downswing time. I am still not quite certain about this since I did not experiment thoroughly enough with a sufficiently wide range of golfers. But I find the matter highly significant (also see Appendix 1) in that when the whip is tuned to the downswing time it is in rhythmic synchronisation with the asymmetry of the flail swing timing. I think this is an effect entirely in the realm of Psycho-Golf but any craftsman knows that for his tools to 'feel right' is of paramount importance.

As of the moment I have an assortment of twelve 1-Woods and I can certainly play best with that one which is tuned at 3.5 cycles to suit my downswing time. Furthermore there is another strange fact about this particular club in that the ball usually goes straight and for this effect I have never found an explanation apart from the bonus inherent in the fact that one's tools 'feel right'.

The major conclusion: the importance of repeating precision – based on Psycho-Golf

In strictly physical terms the most important aspect of the golf stroke is to get a high Strike Efficiency in terms of the first three of the Four Impact Imperatives which specify just what is needed at contact between ball and club. This is emphasised by the fact that one can do almost nothing about that Fourth Impact Imperative as to club speed.

This is illustrated by the formula given earlier in the

$$\text{Golf Stroke Efficiency} + \text{Swing Efficiency} \times \text{Strike Efficiency}$$

It is far more profitable, reflecting on our score, to make a 20 per cent improvement in Strike Efficiency than to attempt to make an (impossible?) improvement of 20 per cent in our Swing Efficiency. The real available leverage for improvement for the Typical Golfer relates to his Strike Efficiency.

But this calls for better *mental grip* and thus we proceed to the third part of this book, which is on the subject of Psycho-Golf.

PART THREE
Psycho-Golf

17
Introduction to Psycho-Golf

In the previous part of the book I have made some novel experiments and have commented on what the results might mean. But when I combine what I have written with my parallel experience on the golf-course as a Typical Golfer I incline to the view that:

> *The Typical golfer is restricted in making further progress by his inability to use his conscious psyche in the most profitable fashion*

I feel convinced that if a good teaching professional knew what went on in the mind of the Typical Golfer struggling with the game on the course he would wring his hands in despair. I think he might also comment: 'How do they manage to make the game so difficult?'

The 'conscious psyche'

First let us be clear what I mean when I use the phrase 'conscious psyche'. I will not strive for some philosophical definition but will restrict the definition to a practical interpretation:

> The conscious psyche is that inner conscious experience as to thoughts and images which might be *communicated* to another person by words or by physical language such as gestures or drawings.

This is a very restricted definition because I have

excluded those other aspects of psyche such as emotions and instincts which tend to be indefinable. But the definition I have given of psyche is the important one for the golfer since it relates to *specific data* (such as 'two and two make four') which is specifically communicable and could be written or illustrated in a book.

Indeed, I will now go further in my restriction of the definition of the conscious psyche so far as the golfer is concerned and declare:

The *useful* conscious psyche for the golfer is that which can be expressed in words.

Why do I further restrict my definition of *'useful golfer's psyche'* to that data which can be expressed in words? Because any other sort of data, instinctive, emotional or imaginative, is in a constant state of subjective flux and such data means one thing on Mondays and another thing on Tuesdays. But verbal data is precise and specific and if I say that 'two and two make four' that statement will hold true for all the days of the week. If our Typical Golfer is to escape from the pitfalls of Golf Mythology (which is based on instinctive-emotional prejudice and fantasy) then the first thing he needs is a precise and unambiguous *language* and for that one cannot beat English literacy.

The human being has made his most rapid and effective progress, especially in science, through the medium of words (or their symbolic equivalent such as mathematical formulae) and I am convinced that rapid and effective progress in golf can only be made in the same fashion. Thus I would define Psycho-Golf as:

Psycho-Golf brings the literate (word) psyche of the golfer to bear on the game as it is played

This is the very opposite of 'robotic golf' for it is 'conscious golf'.

Robotic golf

But if we consider how the Typical Golfer actually plays the game this is concentrated almost entirely in the animal aspect of his central nervous system as shown in Fig. 17.1. This is a matter of the incoming senses telegraphing where the ball is ('eye on the ball') into a skill centre of a nervous reflex nature (the cerebellum) and this actuates instinctive motor reflexes to 'hit the ball'. In this robotic operation there is no need to call on the conscious mind which may well be off-line to what is happening and involved in daydreams which have nothing to do with the game. This is all very well for professional golfers whose skill centre has achieved a high state of effectiveness through arduous practice but it is not good enough for the Typical Golfer.

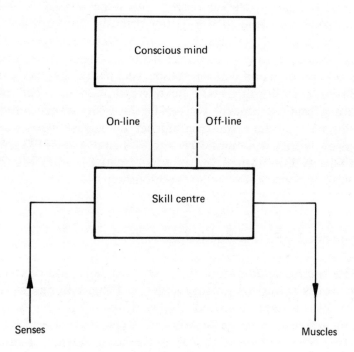

Fig.17.1

The empirical fact appears to be that such robotic golf ('animal golf') is not good enough for the Typical Golfer when the result is measured by a numerical score. It might be good enough in 'relative' games such as tennis where one is only concerned in beating an opponent who may well be less skilled than oneself. But it is not good enough in golf where one is being measured by the actual score of strokes. (I refer to Medal Play which is the more rigorous form of golf.)

When the Typical Golfer has his psyche 'on-line'

The Typical Golfer may well have his conscious (verbal) psyche off-line to the game and be indulging in day-dreams about his business affairs, or his mistress or about the latest cricket scores. But occasionally he has his psyche on-line to the game, actually thinking about it, and this will invariably be 'what went wrong on the last shot and how do I correct it for this next shot?' This is where he runs out of steam because if he has just played a walloping hook he may well decide that 'my stance was too closed' and go for an open stance which may well produce the grandfather of hooks. What goes wrong is that the mental resource of that Typical Golfer is simply not trained to know true cause and effect; he really does not know 'what produces what'.

The need for a true 'mental model'

The mental model of a golfer is what he could describe in words about his golfing skills and this belongs to the conscious (verbal) mind. Now if one joins in a bar conversation with a group of Typical Golfers it is immediately obvious that they all have different mental models of how to play the game and this becomes very clear if one asks them about the most important single feature of their ideas as to how to play the game:

> *Keep one's eye on the ball*
> *Have a good sense of balance*
> *Straight left arm*
> *Hit late*
> *Don't sway*
> > *and so on and so forth.*

This suggests that Typical Golfers *do not have a mental model at all* as to how the game should be played. All they have is a general sense of apprehension and some dubious ideas about how to correct the last bad stroke.

The conditions for a good mental model of golf

If one is to acquire a good and true mental model of golf which will be useful in improving one's game then it must be:

1   Reasonable

The mental model must be based on first principles so that if one has a query it can always be referred back to those first principles. In Part 1, I have given my own view as to the nature of those first principles involving:

Positively – The Four Impact Imperatives.

Negatively – The Five Laws of Cussedness.

This is the prime data on which a mental model should be based.

But also under the heading of 'reasonableness' one must take into account one's personal limitations as to age and physique and establish one's personal targets for Proper Par. This puts the focus upon the importance of Strike Efficiency rather than Swing Efficiency and should orientate us towards accuracy rather than yardage.

2 *Simple*

The Fifth Law of Cussedness is perhaps the most important of all since it calls for mental stretch and if we fail in this then our golf is mindless. But we each have so much natural mental stretch and what we have to do is to *condense the problems* by simplification both physically and mentally so that our mental stretch is adequate to cope with what is fundamental and important. The next chapter deals with this requirement.

3 *Memorable*

A good mental model for golf must be clear and memorable. It is no use having a mental model which is cloudy or has grey edges. It must be as specific as the statement that 'two and two make four'. Only *words* have this degree of specificity but if they are to be memorable they must be curt.

Thus the three main requirements for a good mental model for golf (or anything else) are that it is:

Reasonable
Simple
Memorable

The mental model must be available on-line to the stroke as a Skeleton Model or Golfing Formula

No model is of practical value unless it can be related to real events *now* and that means that a golfing mental model must be available for use during the actual stroke. This implies that there will be two degrees of mental model involved:

a)   An off-line comprehensive model which includes all one's know-how and know-why concerning the game but which is far too large and involved to be of any use during an actual stroke. It has to be kept in the background for reference purposes. It belongs to the armchair rather than the golf course.

b)   An on-line *skeleton model* which has been distilled from the more comprehensive model and which is fully memorable during the golf stroke on the course. In the next chapter I shall propose that such a Skeleton Model should be reduced to three words (relating to the desirable features of Grip, Stance and Swing) so that it becomes a Golfing Formula.

The main objective of Psycho-Golf is to define such a Skeleton Model or Golfing Formula for practical use during our strokes.

18
The Simplicity Postulate
of Science

Psycho-Golf is concerned with getting the best value out of one's brains towards playing a better game. Psycho-Golf is thus as much concerned with *how* one thinks as with what one thinks. The first important overall thought required is to realise that one is faced with a complex ('system') situation and somehow one must reduce it to more simple terms. This means:

1   Every *physical act* related to the golf stroke should be as simple as possible and this particularly relates to the grip, stance and swing.
2   Any *mental model* we construct to help us with the game must also be in the simplest possible form.

Of course, when I use the term 'as simple as possible' I also require that the act, physical or mental, should be effective. Thus what one searches for is *the most effective simplicity*.

In this chapter I consider the reasons for this particular attitude and why effective simplicity is a principle which has to be constantly pursued. My reader may consider that the desirability of the pursuit of simplicity is obvious but I am not at all sure that this is really true.

The Simplicity Postulate of science

Science does not consider that the virtues of simplicity are obvious and it takes this matter so seriously that it has stated:

The Simplicity Postulate is that if one has two solutions to a problem of equal validity, then the simplest will be the best.

Why?

Consider the following equally true statements:

$$2 + 2 = 4 \quad \text{Simpler statement}$$
$$5 + 7 - 8 = 4 \quad \text{More complex statement}$$

The above contains the essence of the Simplicity Postulate since the more complex statement can be *simplified* by reducing the three left-hand terms to two so that we then come out with the statement that $2 + 2 = 4$. Furthermore the nature of the simplification is subtle for we have also reduced the figures of 5,7,8 to the single figure 2. We conclude:

The Simplicity Postulate requires the valid simplification of statements by:
a)   The *elimination* of the irrelevant
b)   The maximum *condensation* of the statement

In this fashion the Simplicity Postulate distils a truth into the briefest and most lucid form so that it finally becomes irreducible.

Nature appears to be based on the Simplicity Postulate

The laws of nature have been unravelled by science using the Simplicity Postulate. This method has been so successful that it appears that each law of nature is itself a manifestation of the Simplicity Postulate. Now what is extraordinary about the laws of nature is not only that they can be represented by the formulae of science but that these formulae are *always triadic*. They always reduce to an ultimate simplicity which has *three factors*. For example:

$E = mc^2$ the main relativity formula showing the simple correlation of mass, energy and the velocity of light

$V^2 = 2as$ the Newtonian formula correlating what velocity a body will reach subject to an acceleration over a given distance

$e = hf$ the main quantum formula correlating energy, frequency and action.

Why *three* terms? Because any two-term statement (such as $V = E$) is a tautology and meaningless. It is only the presence of a third term in a formula which gives it meaning.

The triadic features of the golf-stroke

I have briefly shown from science how much science values the Simplicity Postulate but also how this will always result in an irreducible formula of three independent terms. Now if we consider the golfer we can note two very important aspects of the golf stroke in the need for a balance between:

1   the golfer's swinging of the club as a highly dynamic act . . . the SWING

2   the need for the golfer to have a stable datum rooted to the Earth so that he is not swung off balance . . . the STANCE

But between the swinging of the golf club in the external world of physical reality and the inner need for balance and stability there must be a connection. This connection can only be at the interface between the two aspects and we can define the third aspect:

3   the relationship as between the Swing and the Stance is provided by . . . the GRIP

Thus the most elementary and irreducible simplicity of the golf-stroke is a combination of the three factors of SWING, STANCE and GRIP.

The search for the irreducible simplification of SWING, STANCE and GRIP

I doubt if any golfer would question the above analysis as to the three main factors which are under the golfer's control and each of which must be independently actualised in an effective fashion. But if we keep to the same search for 'effective simplicity' then our search is now narrowing down to finding the answer to the following three questions:

1   What is the most simply effective SWING?
2   What is the most simply effective STANCE?
3   What is the most simply effective GRIP?

The corresponding mental need for simplicity

Thus far I have only considered the strictly physical needs for effective simplicity in the golf stroke and we shall take this study further in later chapters. But since I am advocating Psycho-Golf in which the conscious mind is effectively on-line to the golf stroke then we must also consider the impact of the Simplicity Postulate in the mental sphere. Now we can state our objective:

> **Psycho-Golf requires that we have an easily remembered mental model which will guide us towards effective simplicity as to SWING, STANCE and GRIP.**

I have suggested in the previous chapter that such a model must be a verbal Skeleton Model and thus our quest is to find a *few well chosen words* which will remind us of the important aspects as to SWING, STANCE and GRIP. Such words will then become a basic Golfing Formula.

The simplification of verbal statements

If one is to remember a Skeleton Model consisting of a few words *during the actual golf shot* then the only way it can be memorable is by using as few words as possible and the shortest words possible. We are looking for an 'Open Sesame' to control the golf shot. We have already noted that the Simplicity Postulate requires both the elimination of the irrelevant and the condensation of the relevant.

Example. Imagine I am in my car and looking for the house of a friend. I stop a passer-by and ask him the way and he states:

> 'At the first public house you meet turn left and it is a mile down that road'.

Thus he makes a statement in seventeen words which is quite clear and specific. But I can condense that statement into three words: PUB-LEFT-MILE. Not only does this contain all the relevant instructions, but having only three words I can remember it with ease. But also note that in establishing my formula of PUB-LEFT-MILE I have arranged the words in the correct operational order.

Thus we can be sure that any effective verbal formula has to be brief and specific and arranged in the correct order. The outstanding value of getting the order correct is that one can then concentrate on one word at a time, at its relevant time. Furthermore, such order also informs us what that relevant time is, because this is demarked by the completion of the use of the previous word.

One word per feature

If it is desirable that the verbal description in a Skeleton Model shall be as brief as possible this suggests that each feature as to SWING, STANCE, GRIP should be limited to one word, thus making a total three-word Golfing Formula.

Clearly the words need to be chosen with great care so that they provide the maximum guidance during the golf shot.

We must also be careful to set up the three-word Golfing Formula in the correct order and that will normally be corresponding to GRIP, STANCE, SWING since that is the normal operational golfing order.

The next chapters are essentially a search for an optimum Golfing Formula of three words. I shall try to find the formula which suits me and it is quite possible that my reader would come to a different formula. But what should be common is the search for effective simplicity both in our mental model and in the corresponding physical acts which make up the golf stroke.

The important assumption that one word can programme a phase of physical posture or action

The idea that three words of a Golfing Formula could accurately programme the three main features of the golf stroke as to Grip, Stance and Swing may appear naïve. Ever since the time of St Paul humanity has taken a poor view of the conscious mind concerning its ability to control our physical behaviour.

And yet on the barrack square the sergeant-major has only to pronounce the expression 'RIGHT-WHEEL!' for a hundred men to turn in exact unison and with a high degree of both individual and collective physical skill. If that sergeant-major next produces the word 'HALT!', then all the soldiers come to halt 'as one man'. How is this effect achieved whereby a soldier can perform an exact skilled act through a single command word? It is called 'drill' and consists of:

1 breaking down the possible range of postures and actions into *units* which are relatively self-contained
2 Drilling the unit action by imitation or other instruction until it is automatised
3 Ensuring that the automatised unit action is associated with a trigger word

Thus the soldier is drilled until he has within him an appropriate *Skill Tape* in his skill centre but that tape is set rolling by the appropriate trigger *Drill Word*. The process as a whole may best be described as Word Drill but remembering that the term 'drill' refers to the development of an automatic unit action.

Psycho-Golf is based on sequential word drill

Psycho-Golf is only possible because golf consists of three unit acts (Grip, Stance and Swing) which take place in a sequential order and there is no time limitation (apart from being accused of 'slow play') between the three aspects. Thus in principle one can take as long as one likes in taking one's grip, as long as one likes in taking one's stance and as long as one likes before taking the swing.

This means that if we develop an appropriate drill for each of the three Golfing Formula words, we can concentrate on actualising each word drill as to one word at a time and thus we create a skill situation *by addition* as:

Unit action	*Addition*
GRIP	GRIP
STANCE	GRIP and STANCE
SWING	GRIP and STANCE and SWING

In this fashion Psycho-Golf enables the Typical Golfer to simulate the integrated skill of the professional golfer which has to be learned by hard practice over many years. The Typical Golfer divides the golf stroke into three distinct unit actions each of which is automatised by word drill and the integration by addition takes place by passing along the three word Golfing Formula sequence.

The psychological processes involved in word drill are quite complex and their consideration I have left until Appendix 2 so as not to interfere with the general flow of the book. But I hope my reader will accept the fact from the barracks square that:

*One word can totally and accurately programme
a unit act of physical skill*

19

A Brief Recap as to the Objectives of Psycho-Golf

The last two or three chapters have covered some considerable new ground and it may be desirable to give a brief recap as to the major points involved and the methodology relevant to the next chapters:

1   We start from the assumption that the Typical Golfer cannot improve his inconsistent game because he cannot make enough effective use of his mind.

2   Thus Psycho-Golf is conceived as a new method of golf which trains the mind to be effective during the actual golf stroke. It is suggested that the arduous practice of the professional has to be compensated in the Typical Golfer by better thinking.

3   A fundamental principle we adopt is that 'simplest is best' and this will apply both to the actual physical acts during the golf shot and to the mental model we need of the game.

4   Thus Psycho-Golf is a combination of a general movement towards simplicity together with the need to bring good thinking into play.

5   Whatever general and wide ramifications one may have as to golfing theory there is the need for an extracted Skeleton Model which can be used during the golf stroke itself.

6   This Skeleton Model must be verbal and brief and may best be actualised in a three-word Golfing

Formula corresponding to the three vital aspects of GRIP, STANCE and SWING.

7   In searching for such a Golfing Formula one must bear in mind:

a)   The Four Impact Imperatives.

b)   The Five Laws of Cussedness.

20

The Simplest Possible
Swing

The following chapters will attempt to define that three-word formula relating to GRIP, STANCE and SWING. But before proceeding to them we must first define 'the simplest possible swing' since what one may decide about that reacts on all the three aspects. The objective in achieving the simplest possible swing is not Swing Efficiency nor maximum yardage (although my experience is that it is in no way inferior to other swings in that respect) but rather that the simplest swing will be the most consistently repeatable so that we can 'forget about it' and concentrate on the far more important factor of Strike Efficiency so that we contact the ball squarely, centrally and in-line . . . the first Three Impact Imperatives . . . for *accuracy*!

The swing is a two-link flail

Dr David Williams in his book *The Science of The Golf Swing* demonstrated without a shadow of doubt that the golf swing is a flailing action. In theory one can conceive of an even simpler swing in which the arms and club simply sweep round the shoulders in one straight line like a cricket bat stroke. That is all very well for a heavy object such as a cricket bat but it cannot be used for the golf stroke since the club head is relatively light and must be swung at high speed to develop enough energy to drive the ball its customary distance. But to develop such high club head speeds with the limited speed of the body and arm motion requires that not only must the hands swing round the shoulders but the club head must also swing round the hands.

Any analysis of the golf swing (see also Appendix 1) shows that the club rotates round the hands at twice the angular speed of the hands round the shoulders. This means that the grip of hands on the club is a *hinging grip* and that the total motion is that of a two-link flail with the arms forming the first link in the flail and the club forming the second. This is shown in Fig. 20.1 and the club head speed is given by the formula in the footnote below.

The formula given in the footnote shows conclusively that most of the speed in the club head is provided by the club hinging round the hands in a flailing fashion and only a small fraction is contributed directly by the hand speed as such. Of course all the power for both effects is provided by the body but most of this goes into two-link flailing rather than a simple rotational one-link motion.

Thus we must settle for the concept that the golf swing is a flail action and that this will also apply to 'the simplest possible effective swing'. But given that basic acceptance, then we note that what the golfer must do is to encourage the simplest possible flail action and this occurs when the hands provide a *simple hinging function* and there is no inclination for the hands to be a forceful driving function.

Footnote

Let ω = the angular speed of the hands in the impact area and this is typically 16 radians per second. Assume arm length of 2 feet and effective club length of 3 feet. Therefore typically (for the author):

Club head speed in feet per second

$$= 2\omega + 3 \times 2\omega$$
$$= 2 \times 16 + 3 \times 2 \times 16$$
$$= 32 + 96$$
$$= 128 \text{ ft sec.}$$

Furthermore, if the swing is a two-link flail then the 'hand' which is powering the flail must be the shoulders since any two-link flail must be driven from its inboard extremity . . . and that is the shoulders. This is not an easy concept to grasp since we are used to thinking of the actual hands as the power-point in golf. But the arms are only one link in a two-link mechanics and the power-point can only be the shoulders. I recap:

1   The true interface as between the golfer and the golfing mechanics is the shoulders since this is the 'hand' powering the two-link flail.

2   Thus the sense of human golfing power-source must be associated with the shoulders and not the hands or arms. The hands-arms are a mere kinetical linking system.

The simple proof of this analysis is that it does not affect the power into the golf club whether the hands hold the club lightly or tightly. Indeed, it has been stated that the grip of Jack Nicklaus is about the same as he would use in shaking hands with a young child. The only functional requirement by the hands is that they should *hinge* and thus provide the central hinge in a two-link flail.

The search for simplicity in a two-link flail swing

We must accept that the golf swing is a two-link flailing action and thus we next seek to find the simplest fashion in which such a two-link flail can be actualised. My analysis of the over-riding considerations is:

1   The 'hand' which powers the flail is the shoulders

2   The first link in the flail is the *left* arm since on the backswing the right arm must fold around its elbow and 'get out of the way'

3   The hands must act as a mere *hinge*, the hinge between the first flail link of the left arm and the second flail link of the club

This focuses attention upon:

The *Shoulders* . . . as the means for providing flail power

The *Left arm* . . . as the first flail-link within the golfer's body

The *Hands* . . . as the hinge in the two-link flail

Now what all this should tell us is that:

a)   When considering the focus of *power* in the golf-stroke, this should be focused in the shoulders.

b)   When it comes to considering the kinematics (motional mechanics) of the golf stroke this will involve:

(i)   a *straight left arm* as the golfer's contribution to the first (inboard) link of the two-link flail.

(ii)   the hand and wrists as a mere *hinge* as between the two elements (arms and club) of that two-link flail.

These three fundamental facts about the golf swing are illustrated in Fig. 20.1.

The central significance of the shoulders

In earlier chapters on the subject of the difference between Speed and Power Golfers I have analysed that golfing power has two sources. There is a Body-Twist which provides access to about 80 per cent of the total body muscle power, although this is mainly 'slow' muscle, and there is a residual 20 per cent associated with Shoulder-Arm Rock which appears to be fast muscle and therefore more efficient as to Swing Efficiency. Thus although the total power in the Shoulder-Arm Rock is potentially small compared with that in the Body-Twist, yet its significance is appreciable when one takes fast muscle efficiency into consideration. But what is most significant in this situation is that *the shoulders*

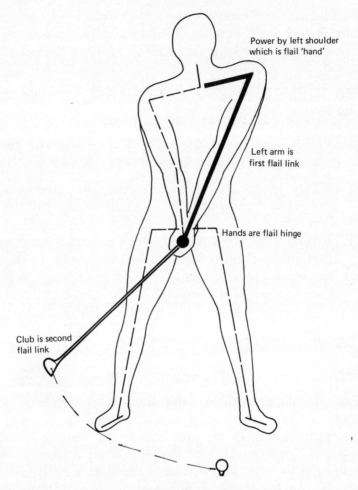

Power by left shoulder
which is flail 'hand'

Left arm is
first flail link

Hands are flail hinge

Club is second
flail link

Fig.20.1

are common to both parts of the golfer's power. On the
one hand the shoulders are the end-point of the Body-
Twist and on the other hand they are the starting point
of the Shoulder-Arm Rock.

I raise this matter to pin-point the centrality of the
shoulders as to the powering aspect of the golf swing and
this point is very relevant when we also take into

consideration the fact that the shoulders are the 'power-point' in treating the swing as a two-link flail.

That Fourth Law of Cussedness: Wrist Cocking and Arm Rolling (see Fig. 20.2).

If one built a golfing machine which incorporated a flail two-link swing the hinge between the two links would only be permitted to hinge in the swing arc and would not be permitted to rotate along the swing plane since that would take the club face off-square. This phenomenon as applied to the human golfer we considered in Chapter 5 as the Fourth Law of Cussedness and I repeat briefly what can happen.

As the club is approaching the top of the backswing the wrists first hinge correctly along the swing arc, but due to the residual swing momentum in the club head this will extend any further possibility of human body motion. The latter is the ability of the wrists to cock (beyond hinging), but to keep the club head on the swing arc this requires that the arms roll clockwise and the club face opens related to its former squareness to the swing arc. Thus the club face is now lying along the club head swing arc instead of square to it and this fact can readily be seen if, at the end of the backswing, the toe of the club is pointing to the ground. But this effect can be as much as 90 degrees off-square and somehow this has to be restored on the downswing by anti-clockwise unrolling of the arms.

But the chance of restoration of squareness is remote and thus the club face will contact the ball with some degree of unwanted open-ness or shut-ness. One is relying on the fact that the arms will unroll in the downswing to the precise degree they have rolled clockwise in the backswing. But whilst there was a specific force of club momentum creating the rolling of

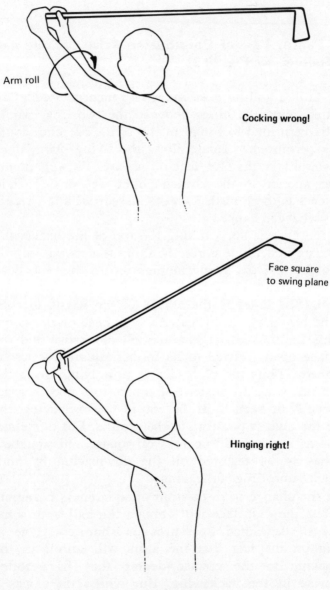

Fig.20.2

the arms on the backswing, there is no equivalent specific unrolling force on the downswing and any unrolling relies upon an instinctive feel that the hands are getting into a true hitting position.

This phenomenon is acknowledged by good golfers and the result has been to develop towards the so-called 'square' method of backswing so that the club face is encouraged to keep more square to the swing arc throughout. But in practice the square method only goes part of the way and although it reduces arm rolling it does not eliminate it. Nevertheless the majority of top professionals and amateurs now use this square method.

My own view is that this so-called square method does not go far enough in ensuring accurate squareness of the club face at impact and that the important improvement to be made is to keep the club face really square to the swing arc through the swing and this can only be done by limiting the wrist motion to hinging and by totally inhibiting wrist-cocking and the consequent arm-rolling.

I call this recommended swing The Hinge-Square Swing.

The simplest possible swing – 'The Hinge-Square Swing'

The Hinge-Square Swing thus has the following analysis:

1   It is a two-link flail swing having the components:
     a)   The left arm is the upper link of the flail
     b)   The wrists are the hinge of the flail
     c)   The club is the lower link of the flail

2   The 'hand' which is powering the flail swing is mainly the left shoulder which is also the common centre of co-ordination between the Body-Twist and the Shoulder-Arm Rock. But the driving power from

the left shoulder has to be transmitted via the left hand and thus the most important golfing limb is the left arm from shoulder to hand. I shall call this 'The Left Arm Imperative'.

3   During the backswing the wrist motion (as the flail hinge) must be limited to the hinging mode and we shall later note that there is a preferred grip to encourage this.

The effect of using the Hinge-Square Swing is to give a remarkable improvement in directional accuracy due to meeting that First Impact Imperative that the club face must be square to the swing arc at impact. The swing is shorter than the normal cocking swing, but since the main body motion (apart from the wrists) is unchanged, I have found no loss of length or of swing speed measured on DOC. There is a final bonus in the Hinge-Square Swing if one benefits from using whippy clubs as they are only fully effective with this swing. If one uses a full cocking swing the club has to rotate 90 degrees in the downswing and thus the whip axis is also rotating instead of just whipping along the club swing arc. Dr David Williams has cited this latter fact as one reason why whippiness does not work. But using the Hinge-Square Swing whippiness can be fully effective.

We now start that quest for a three-word Golfing Formula in earnest having decided it will relate to the Hinge-Square Swing.

21

The Grip
(Formula Word 'Thumb')

We now start our quest to find those three Golfing Formula words corresponding to GRIP-STANCE-SWING and we start with GRIP.

The correct form of grip will depend upon the decided form of swing and since I have settled for the Hinge-Square Swing this provides the main clue as to the desirable associated GRIP. What we need is a GRIP which will encourage hinging and discourage cocking.

Experiment. Put your hands together and find in which mode they collaborate best as to hinging along the swing arc. The answer is simple and unambiguous.

> *The wrists hinge most freely when the hand PALMS are facing each other*

Second experiment. Grip the two hands together as strongly as possible. What does one observe?

> *The grip is strongest when the hand PALMS are facing each other*

Third experiment. Keep the hands together as above in a common grip but now also hinge the wrists to left and right. If the grip is too strong the hinging effect is limited because the grip muscles tense the wrists. But if the grip is relaxed the hands can hinge as much as if they were separated.

Now we want a maximum hinging effect, i.e. with palms facing each other, but we also need to have a grip which is firm but does not inhibit hinging. This can only be the grip with the palms facing each other since that is inherently the strongest grip and thus has the maximum capacity for relaxation without becoming loose. Hence:

Only a palm-to-palm grip permits easy wrist-hinging with adequate holding firmness

Thus I shall call this grip the PALM-TO-PALM grip.

Taking up the Palm-to-Palm Grip (See Fig. 21.1)

The palm-to-palm grip has to be taken up symmetrically, i.e. without any wrist rolling, but when holding a club the palm-to-palm effect is staggered by the different points where the left and right hands are located. But that does not change the beneficial properties of the grip. As to the type of grip (two-handed, overlapping, interlocking) I think this is a matter for individual preference and habit and none of them interferes with the palm-to-palm principle.

But now there comes a nice bonus because it happens that with the palm-to-palm grip taken symmetrically (without wrist rolling) the thumb of the left hand lies down that central mark on the club grip which is provided by the club makers to indicate that the club face is square to the swing line when that mark is uppermost.

Thus the key first act in taking up the palm-to-palm grip is:

First place the left thumb down the centre
of the shaft grip on top of the marked
centre-line

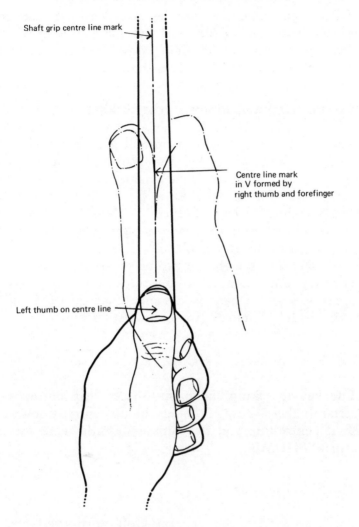

Shaft grip centre line mark

Centre line mark
in V formed by
right thumb and forefinger

Left thumb on centre line

Fig.21.1

If one does that then one finds that automatically the palm is square to the swing arc (and the back of the left hand is pointing towards the required strike objective such as the flag). One will also note that with this grip *no knuckles of the left hand are showing.*

The right hand can then be placed on the club grip with its palm facing the left hand and also with the 'V' between thumb and forefinger down the centre of the shaft and also with no knuckles showing.

How the left thumb inhibits wrist-cocking

If we take a stance with a normal grip in which both hands are somewhat over the grip and with the two thumbs also somewhat each side of the club grip centre-line this establishes a grip which encourages wrist-cocking due to absence of thumb control. But wrist-cocking with the palm-to-palm grip would take place against the left thumb since it takes place along the swing arc. The left thumb can be sensitive to detect this tendency and hold it in check. Overall we have a situation with the hand palms encouraging wrist-hinging while the left thumb discourages wrist-cocking.

The Formula Word 'THUMB'

The key to taking the palm-to-palm grip correctly is certainly the placing of the left thumb centrally down the shaft centre-line and the simple formula word for the grip is 'THUMB'.

The First Formula

We started with the general Golfing Formula as to GRIP-STANCE-SWING and we are now looking for one word corresponding to each of these three aspects and one which will remind us as to the chief desirable feature. Having selected the first word THUMB for the GRIP the formula is first:

'THUMB'-STANCE-SWING

22
The Stance
(Formula Word 'Skilt')

The word 'stance' implies both a correct stable standing posture before the ball and also a correct lining up of the ball to the club (sometimes called The Address).

The Three Laws of Cussedness involved

The Stance is the most important of the three main golfing factors since it is directly involved with Three Laws of Cussedness:

First Law. The problem of Hand Asymmetry in that the need to take the grip with the right hand lower than the left involves a basic asymmetric distortion of the body.

Second Law. The fact that the golfer has to take his stroke in a side-swiping arc to one side of him means that there is only one correct position for the ball if it is to be contacted in the desired direction of strike.

Third Law. The problem of Jelly-on-Springs and the three varieties of sway or bounce which this can create and thus lower Strike Efficiency.

The Ski-Stance for Jelly-on-Springs: Vertical Bounce

If the golfer 'bounces' during the stroke he will either top the ball or hit the ground behind the ball according to whether he was bouncing up or down at the time.

This severely reduces his Strike Efficiency. Vertical bounce was considered quantitatively in Chapter 13 and we noted that it was due to excessive knee bending, but that it is negligible if the knees are only cracked forwards by not more than two inches. Such a limited degree of knee bending is quite compatible with the general knee flexibility one needs for the swing. It implies that the overall stance should be rather 'stood up' and free from crouching. I delay the exact description of the requisite Ski-stance to a little later since it also has to cope with Side-Sway.

The Ski-Stance for Jelly-on-Springs: Side-Sway

The legs and feet, including knees, have no slackness of their own to provide side-sway motion. Side-sway is the leading cause of hitting the ground before the ball and thus causing loss of yardage. Side-sway is due to a freedom in the hip joints combined with rolling motion of the ankles and it is possible because the two hip-joints and the two ankle-joints form the four corners of a quadrilateral which has no basic stability like a triangle. We have seen from Chapter 13 that the easy slack motion in the system is some seven inches from centrality.

In order to avoid side-sway one has to stiffen up the quadrilateral by tensing the inside muscles of the legs, particularly of the thighs, while at the same time bringing the knees towards each other and rolling the ankles onto the inner edge of the feet so that they are brought towards their end-stops.

This is approximately the ski-stance adopted by snow skiers as shown in Fig. 22.1 and is a stance of maximum postural stability and almost completely eliminates side-sway. One can sway from such a posture but only consciously and this is why it is used as the datum posture by snow-skiers from which they can make conscious excursions. The side-sway is inhibited essentially by the tensing of the inside thigh-muscles which need to be relaxed for side-sway to take place.

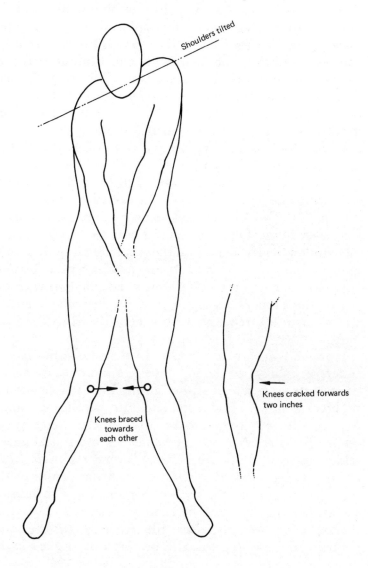

Fig.22.1

The auxiliary feature for Jelly-on-Springs as to Forward-Sway

The third feature of swaying or bouncing due to Jelly-on-Springs is that of forwards sway by the golfer towards the ball (or backwards sway). This is a frequent source of hitting the ball with the club toe due to backwards sway and less frequently to hitting the ball with the club heel due to forwards sway. The main phenomenon is as follows. As the club head comes towards impact it has a centrifugal force of about 80 pounds which is pulling the golfer towards the ball in forwards sway. If the golfer is somewhat off balance and lets his weight go onto the balls of the feet, then his club also moves forwards (across the line of strike) and he will hit the ball with the heel of the club (or 'shank'). However, in most cases the golfer will not be off balance. He automatically reacts to the centrifugal pull of the club by rocking back on his heels, in which case the club is drawn inboards the golfer will strike the ball with the toe of the club. This is not a conscious effect and is simply a reflex reaction to the centrifugal pull of the club.

However, we saw in Chapter 13 that the golfer has an indeterminancy of some four inches of forwards-backwards sway whilst still retaining his balance and the problem is how to find a stable datum within this range. My conclusion is to make use of the stability of end-stops as considered in Chapter 13 and this suggests taking up the stance with the *weight on the heels* when correctly aligned to the ball, i.e. with the centre of the club head opposite the ball at the address. Providing a golfer keeps a natural balance which will have him rocked back on his heels in reacting to the club centrifugal forces, he will still be correctly aligned to the ball at impact.

Summary of Ski-Stance for counteracting Jelly-on-Springs

Thus the overall interpretation of the Ski-Stance is:

> *Take the ski-stance to avoid both sidesway and vertical bounce. But also take it with the main body weight on both heels when lining up to the ball to deal with forwards sway.*

The above accounts for the component SKI in the overall Formula Word SKILT for dealing with the stance.

TILT the shoulders for correct hand asymmetry compensation

We next consider that First Law of Cussedness which distorts the golfer's body due to having to grip the club with the right hand lower than the left. There are two alternative methods whereby we can get both hands on the club:

The shoulder twisting method

If we move the right shoulder forwards (towards the ball), as shown in Fig. 22.2, and the left shoulder backwards this effectively lengthens the right arm compared with the left arm and we can get both hands upon the club. But in doing so we have twisted the shoulders in an horizontal plane so that our stance is now 'open'. Now it is well established that it is the line made by the two shoulders at impact which defines the club swing plane direction and with such an open stance the downswing plane will be from out-to-in and the club head will cut across the ball and cause a slice.

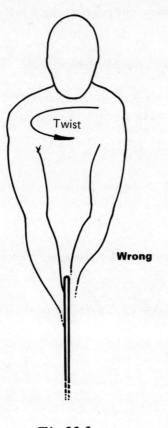

Fig.22.2

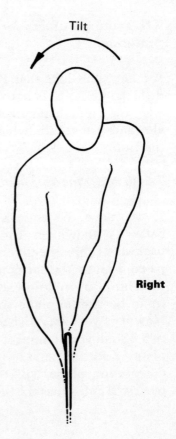

Fig. 22.3

The shoulder tilting method

Alternatively we can get both hands on the club by tilting the shoulders as shown in Fig. 22.3 so that the right shoulder is lowered and the left shoulder is raised. It is achieved by a single tilting motion from the hips combined with a re-balancing of the feet as shown in Fig. 5.1. This is the correct method because it leaves the shoulders in line with the square strike direction to the flag.

Thus the correct adjustment is:

> *To correct for hand asymmetry on the club, the shoulders are tilted by moving the hips to the left whilst keeping even weight balance on both feet.*

Summary of the formula word 'SKILT' for the stance

The correct stance is summarised in the Golfing Formula Word 'SKILT' which is made up from two contributions:

SKI   take up a ski-type stance as described to avoid bouncing or side-sway but combine it with having the body weight on the heels to avoid forwards-backwards sway.

(T)ILT   Tilt the shoulders to get the two hands correctly on the club while keeping the shoulders parallel to the desirable strike line.

Thus:

SKI + TILT = SKILT

Our original general Golfing Formula of GRIP-STANCE-SWING has now developed to THUMB-SKILT-SWING and we have one final word to consider in relation to SWING.

23
The Swing
(Formula Word 'Brush')

A very subtle matter!

To find a Golfing Formula word to represent the Swing and in such a fashion as to be useful to the golfer as he plays his stroke has proved the most elusive of all my quests. But I think I may have elucidated the *nature of the problem*. What we are looking for must be a word to define the desirable swing plane. This definition is not inherent in deciding in favour of that simplest Hinge-Square Swing for this can be played in several alternative swing planes. I think the nature of the problem is:

1   The swing has two power sources:
  a)   A Body-Twist in a horizontal plane
  b)   A Shoulder-Arm Rock in a vertical plane
2   The actual swing plane will be inclined and is a combination ('vector addition') of the above two factors but there is nothing in the human body which can detect the nature of this combination.

Experiment (see also Fig. 23.1) Take a club such as a 1-Wood and take it back on the first two feet of the backswing in two distinct fashions:
a)   By a body motion which is pure Body-Twist with no Shoulder-Arm Rock. It will be noted that the path of the club immediately comes 'inside the line' and

151

keeps close to the ground. Even after a full hip and shoulder turn the club is only some ten inches above the ground. See 'A' of Fig. 23.1.

b) By a body motion which is pure Shoulder-Arm Rock with no Body-Twist. It will be noted that the path of the club stays on the strike line and is in a vertical arc. See 'B' of Fig. 23.1.

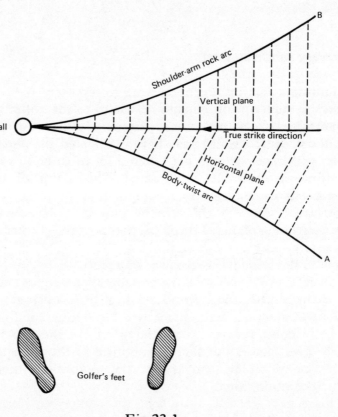

Fig.23.1

The above two experiments will quickly prove that the two sources of golf power, both centred in the shoulders, are utterly different and it is clear that the swing plane is a composite and that it will change accordingly as we vary the proportion of Body-Twist or Shoulder-Arm Rock. Note that the composite actual swing plane has no fixed geometrical basis that we could assign to any specific body motion. Indeed the motion of the left shoulder is a sort of skew spiral.

The 'Takeaway' geometrical motion as the only 'Fact'

We are thus faced with a composite motion of the club head in the backswing which is partly a horizontal motion and partly a vertical motion and thus we have a highly indeterminate swing plane. But fortunately we have one key instrumental fact in the situation and that is the observed motion of the club head in the takeaway part of the backswing. It is this takeaway motion which defines ('instruments') the actual swing plane and thus we can set the backswing on a variety of swing planes simply by controlling the nature of the takeaway motion at the start of the backswing. For example, if I lead the club head in a plane close to the ground this will establish a flattish swing plane whereas if I take the club sharply upwards this will create a more vertical plane.

But which of the two do I want, or which compromise do I want?

Now we note two things:
a)   The Body-Twist arc comes back inside the line
b)   The Shoulder-Arm Rock keeps to the line but *does not go outside it*

This means that if we accept the composite plane as normal (and we have no choice about this) then the composite arc should come back inside the line. It should come back inside the line less than that of a pure Body-Twist takeaway but more than a Shoulder-Arm Rock takeaway.

Thus:

*In deciding the correct takeaway in the back-
swing the only valid choice is the degree to which
the takeaway comes back inside the strike line*

Note that the one impermissible takeaway would be one
which went back outside the strike line. This bad effect
is rather difficult to judge because the Shoulder-Arm
Rock *looks* as if it is going outside the strike line on
takeaway, which it need not. It is an optical illusion in
that lifting a club in takeaway from the strike line shows
a space between club and line below which *appears* to
imply an in-to-out takeaway.

It is all a horrible dilemma and in seeking a solution I
have studied one constant in the matter which occurs if
one uses a takeaway which touches the ground for the
first few inches (the 'brushing' takeaway) and which
relies on the presence of the ground to act as some sort
of stable reference geometrical datum. All one can say
about such a takeaway is that it is stable and will define a
specific swing plane (perhaps on the flatish side since it
is biassed towards the flat Body-Twist arc). But is it any
use? Now oddly enough I find that this worked for me
and I think the sense in the situation is that at least one
has a specific method to define a specific plane but also
that even the vertical Shoulder-Arm Rock plane brushes
the ground for a certain distance of about four inches. By
contrast the purely Body-Twist arc can brush the ground
for some two feet before it begins to lift off the ground a
little.

But the fact that a vertical arc will brush the ground
for about four inches and that a quasi-horizontal arc will
brush the ground for a much longer distance, means that
we could have a method for adjusting the relative
components to the actual swing plane by:

*Brushing the club along the ground in takeaway
can be used to determine the swing plane*

inasmuch as we continue the brushing action for more than four inches. The degree to which we brush the ground more than four inches will determine the relative flatness of the swing and the degree to which the Body-Twist power will dominate over the Shoulder-Arm Rock power.

The degree of ground brushing at takeaway must be personal

I am convinced that 'ground brushing' by the club head in the backswing takeaway is the only known means of defining a given swing plane since if we do not use the ground as a fixed reference datum there is no other datum available. But the amount or length of such brushing action will depend very much on the physique of the individual golfer. If one is a Power Golfer (such as myself) one needs to use the maximum of Body-Twist power and this is encouraged by a flatter swing plane and thus a longer phase of ground brushing. In my own case I find about eight inches is good for me.

The great advantage of ground brushing as an aid to defining the swing (through its swing plane) is that it is as specific as 'two and two make four'.

The Golfing Formula word for the swing is 'BRUSH'

I spent about six months in experiments to find a single Golfing Formula word which might be useful in the golf swing. I realised that it had to relate to the slow start to the backswing since thereafter things go too quickly for verbal control. I was also convinced that we had to seek a solution which had the effect of starting the backswing on a correct plane.

Thus the Golfing Formula word is BRUSH but how much brushing is a matter for personal decision.

Our total Golfing Formula, our Skeleton Model, which commenced as GRIP-STANCE-SWING now becomes:

THUMB-SKILT-BRUSH

24

The Final Correctives

Psycho-Golf as so far described in terms of a general aim towards simplicity and the use of a three-word Golfing Formula does not of itself help a golfer to play well but it gives him a basic *consistency*.

But the formula for good golf is:

$$\text{Good Golf} = \text{Basic Consistency} + \text{Final Correctives.}$$

If a golfer has a basically simple style which 'repeats' as to results then all that is finally required are a few correctives based on what happens on the golf course. The chief feature of Psycho-Golf is a method to achieve consistency and it does not matter if the result is consistent slicing or hooking or other consistent fault for these are easily put right by the Final Correctives. Such final correctives do not mean that there is anything wrong with the golfer's style but are very much due to the fact that we have not yet dealt with that Second Law of Cussedness in that the swing is a side swipe in an arc and there is only one point on that arc where the club is travelling in the same direction as the required direction of ball flight. This affects two things in that if one is striking the ball away from the Tangential Point then this will cause slicing or hooking due to cutting across the ball, and it may also cause the club face to be a little open or shut at impact.

The eight main deviations from the straight shot

It is how one cuts across the ball and whether the club face is open or shut which gives rise to the eight main deviations from the straight shot and these are given in Fig. 24.1. They can all be corrected by two means:

1 By moving the position of the ball relative to the feet forwards or backwards along the strike line
2 By opening or closing the club face at the address by a minor modification of the grip

In Fig. 24.1 are shown the causes of the eight deviations and the nature of their cure. In two cases it is only necessary to change the grip (for simple pushing or pulling) while in two other cases it is only necessary to change the ball position (for slicing or hooking). But in four cases it is necessary to make the double correction (for the push-slice, pull-slice, push-hook and pull-hook). But note that all these eight main deviations can be corrected either by a change of ball position or of grip or both.

Ball position correction for hooking or slicing

The first matter to tackle is any tendency to slice or hook due to ball spin by cutting across the line of strike at impact whether or not the deviation is simple or compounded with pushing and pulling. It is a mistake to try to correct two things at once.

The correction for slicing or hooking is shown in Fig. 24.2 which shows three characteristic swing arcs at AA, BB and CC. Each of us will develop a characteristic swing arc and *this must be left alone*. In Fig. 24.2 it is also shown that there is a correct ball position for each swing arc. If you are Mr AA then you need the ball at X,

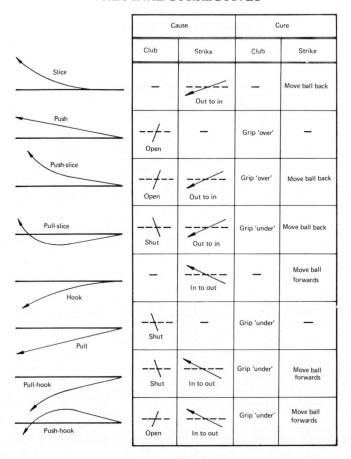

Fig.24.1

if you are Mr BB you want the ball at Y, while if you are Mr CC you should have it at Z. This correct ball location can only be found by trial and error and it should lie in the range between opposite the left toe and six inches inboard from this position. If one requires a correction outside this range then one needs to check back on that Golfing Formula and particularly as to whether one is tilting the shoulders properly so that they are parallel to the correct line of flight.

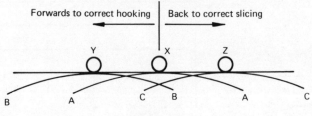

Fig. 24.2

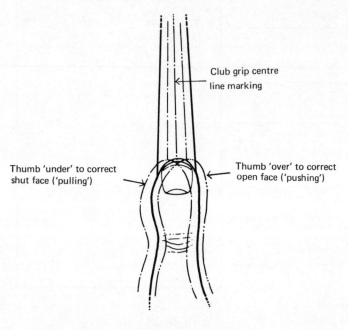

Fig. 24.3

Grip (left thumb) correction for pushing or pulling

Pushing (a straight ball which goes to the right) or
pulling (a straight ball which goes to the left) can only be
due to having the club face open or shut respectively at
impact. This is corrected by bringing the left thumb
further over the shaft to close the face to correct pushing

and the opposite for the correction of pulling. (See Fig. 24.3.) Note that one adheres to the palm-to-palm grip so that both hands now have a slightly different alignment with regard to the centre-line mark on the shaft grip. But having taken the new correcting grip the new notional centre-line should be brought onto the top of the shaft for central alignment. In this fashion the club face witnessed at the address will be seen to be a trifle closed for push correction and a trifle open for pull correction. But one should note that the change of grip, as due to a change in the alignment of the left thumb related to the club centre-line mark, should be quite small. One should not experiment with a shift of more than $\frac{1}{8}$ inch at any time since even this is equal to over a ten degree change in the club face angle. Indeed, I think that incremental changes of $\frac{1}{16}$ inch are enough and we are warned how important is the accuracy with which we take the grip related to its centre-line markings. All clubs should be checked to ensure that the grip centre-line markings are central when the club face is square.

The search for simplicity – eliminate mannerisms

One source of quite unnecessary complexity in the golf stroke is mannerisms. If one sees a Typical Golfer with well marked mannerisms one can be fairly sure he will play inconsistently because the mannerisms are occupying psychic functions which should be used to concentrate on the shot. My own experience is that one would do well to eliminate all the following:

Practice swing
Preparatory waggles
Undue feet shufflings at the address

One simply cannot play Psycho-Golf if one is disturbed by such things.

The search for simplicity – the feet alignment

The foot position affects the takeaway arc with a closed stance favouring a flatter swing inside the strike line and an open stance producing a more vertical swing and perhaps going outside the strike line ('slicing'). These are not absolute laws but are of signficance when taken together with the other facts which can affect takeaway. I found again that 'simplest is best' and that it is simpler to have one's toes in a line parallel to the strike line, neither open nor closed, and thus leaving the correction of hooks, slices, pushes and pulls to the corrective measures I have already suggested. There are twenty different ways of curing a slice or hook but what is important is to analyse what is simplest and especially with regard to its interference with other aspects. At all costs one has to get rid of 'correction and counter correction' such as (for example) hitting a straight ball by combining a hooker's grip with a slicer's stance.

It is for such reasons that in this book I have concentrated directly on those Four Impact Imperatives and those Five Laws of Cussedness which are fundamental to the game and are objective facts.

Accounting for the Laws of Cussedness and the Impact Imperatives

I now summarise how I have dealt in Part 3 with all those Five Laws of Cussedness and the Four Impact Imperatives:

Five Laws of Cussedness	*Golfing Formula or Final Corrective*
1 Hand asymmetry	TILT the shoulders as reminded by the SKILT word for the Stance
2 Ground arc	Ball position as Final Corrective
3 Jelly-on-Springs	SKI stance and weight on heels as in the SKILT word for Stance
4 Wrist cocking and arm rolling	By developing the Hinge-Square swing for simplicity and the correct grip as to THUMB grip formula word.
5 The system complexity problem	Both by pursuing simplicity in the swing and in the mental model of a curt Golfing Formula
Four Impact Imperatives 1 Square face	By using the Hinge-Square swing and the THUMB grip and with a final corrective to the latter if needed
2 Centrality	By taking the Stance with the weight on the heels as an associated item of SKILT
3 Straight impact	By the TILT aspect of SKILT for the stance which ensures the shoulders are parallel to the required strike direction

4 Adequate club-head speed

There is little one can do about this as it is innate in a golfer. But the Hinge-Square swing helps consistency

25
The Two Stages of Psycho-Golf

When I was progressively developing the Golfing Formula on the golf course I had a rather interesting experience which convinced me of a certain subtlety in the matter. I had put aside a whole two weeks in which I resolved to play one round a day and with the thought that if one could not master Psycho-Golf over fourteen rounds, then it must be a dead loss.

My commencing rounds were about 95 shots but these came down over seven days to my best round of 77 shots. Then a strange thing happened in that my scores began to rise until on the fourteenth round I took 105 strokes. I had finished worse than I started, although in the middle I had played to about ten shots better than my handicap.

What did it mean? In the event I found out exactly what it meant and when I had the answer I was able to go out again and score to single figures.

My first impression was that after playing a round a day for fourteen days in succession I was tired and 'over-golfed' but in fact I was not all that tired and I formulated a different proposition as follows:

Psycho-golf with its conscious focus in the word-mind can eventually confuse the 'natural golfer' in one so that it gives up and one is left with all words and no physical skills

Eventually this proved to be the true explanation and I

think it important to understand the matter if one is to benefit from Psycho-Golf and not be put off by it by my sort of experience of going stale.

My full explanation is as follows:

1   Each of us has within him two sorts of golfer:

    a)   A Natural Golfer who has been playing the game for years and enjoying it with all its frustrations

    b)   A Psycho-Golfer who theorises about the game and is constantly making experiments, particularly related to trying to correct the last bad shot

I think most Typical Golfers present a reasonable balance between these two sides of themselves and this balance I show in Fig. 25.1.

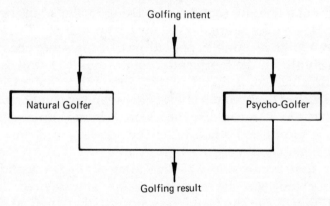

Fig.25.1

2   If one concentrates on the mental aspect of Psycho-Golf at the expense of our Natural Golfer then this balance becomes lost and one is 'all theory and no practice'. This leads to the situation shown in Fig. 25.2 in which our Natural Golfer virtually 'vanishes'. But the Psycho-Golfer cannot play at all

without the natural imagination and skill of the Natural Golfer and so our game collapses. This is the time when we think we are over-golfed and should lay off for a bit. But that is not the real answer to the situation.

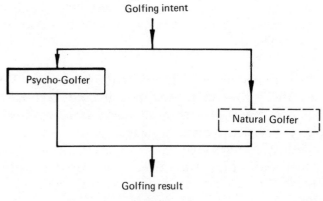

Fig.25.2

3   The next requirement is that we rectify the imbalance by 'promoting' our Natural Golfer while at the same time 'diminishing' our Psycho-Golfer and only using that degree of Psycho-Golf which is beginning to be automatised in our Skill-Tapes and is shown in Fig. 25.3. This means there has to be a

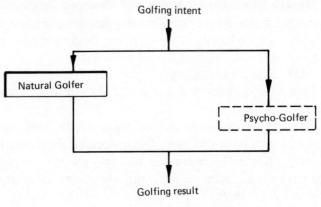

Fig.25.3

change in the main focus of our attention from 'the head' towards 'the body'. This does not mean we have to forget what we may have learned from Psycho-Golf but we have to realise that *actual* golf can only be played by our Natural Golfer and that the true role of Psycho-Golf has been to provide some good habits at the expense of bad habits and mannerisms.

When I had formulated this explanation to myself I went out on the golf course and put it into practice and completely regained my best golf. This means that Psycho-Golf has two distinct stages:

a)   there is a first stage when we are *learning* Psycho-Golf and which will give good initial results but these will fade after a time as we become 'word-bound'

b)   there has to be a second stage when Golfing Formulae as such are allowed to drift to the back of the mind and we only use that degree which has already automatised in our physical posture and actions whilst at the same time encouraging our Natural Golfer to dominate the situation.

This does not mean that the Golfing Formula has vanished but rather that it has changed its essential nature from words into muscular imagination and when this happens then we are beginning to play more in the fashion of a professional.

Of course we always have the verbal Golfing Formula in reserve if our game threatens to creak a little.

The change from Stage a) to Stage b) is basically a *change of attitude*, a change of emotional valuation. In a very early chapter I contrasted the two main viewpoints about golf as to 'Naturalists' and 'Analysts' and stated my personal preference for the latter and this is the zone of Psycho-Golf as I have described it. But in retrospect I think we have to find a more subtle compromise in treating Analysis as a very important *learning mode* of golf while conceding that the ultimate actual golf has to be played by our Natural Golfer.

The transition to three points of judgment

The basic Golfing Formula (such as THUMB-SKILT-BRUSH) is entirely analytical as to the cultivation of desirable robotims in the three main golfing aspects of Grip, Stance and Swing. But with the shift to the second phase of Psycho-Golf these should be replaced (not abandoned) by three aspects of *judgment* by the Natural Golfer in us. Our Natural Golfer lives in the world of imagination (in a real sense) and in judgments associated with such imagination. It is my experience that the Golfing Formula should now develop into Three Judgments as to:

1   *Squareness* We make a final observation and judgment that the club face is lying squarely behind the ball. If it is not we make an instinctive slight modification of the angle we are holding the club (not taking a new grip).

2   *Balance* There has to be a second judgment that we are well balanced and have the general feeling that we are ideally poised to hit the ball. This feeling is not analytical but is total and organic and is perhaps the central desirable feature of the imagination and judgment of our Natural Golfer.

3   *Strike-mood* The final judgment relates to our Strike-Mood as a sort of hitting-intent. For myself I like a Strike-Mood which I would call 'Middling' in that I feel neither too aggressive nor too relaxed. This is a matter for individual judgment but I am certain the strike-mood is of great importance and

relates to the golfer's 'type'. For example if one tends to be physically lazy then one may have to 'work oneself up a little' whereas if one tends to be over-exuberant or rash then perhaps the better strike-mood involves a little restraint.

Thus we can compare the nature of the first and second phases of Psycho-Golf as:

Aspect	First stage Verbal Analytical-Mental	Second stage Judgments Natural Golfer
Grip	THUMB	SQUARENESS
Stance	SKILT	BALANCE
Swing	BRUSH	STRIKE-MOOD

It should be noted that the second stage does not take place in the 'thinking' mind nor does it require the use of any words. It takes place entirely in the world of instinctive sensing and feelings and when highly developed it becomes one strike judgment . . . the Natural Golfer. But by this time the first stage should have done its work so that there is an acquired foundation of good habits or 'robotisms' which assure us of basically correct technique on which can next be superimposed that most vital Natural Golfer in us.

Appendix 1
Club Whip and
the Flail Swing

The purpose of this appendix is to elaborate on the problem of club whippiness considered in Chapter 14. In that chapter I came to the view that all golfers were sensitive to club whip and appeared to prefer a club whose whip cycle time was about the same as their downswing time. I also noted personally that I could hit a ball further with a club of such characteristics but I concluded that this was psychological in that one can swing a club faster when it 'feels right'. In this appendix I attempt to establish the basis of what is involved in 'feeling right'.

A new wave analysis of the downswing

If one studies the step-by-step downswing analyses published in such books as *The Search for The Perfect Swing* (Heinemann) one can derive the acceleration or force curve which is typically as in Fig. A1. The curve is asymmetrical and peaks at about three-quarters through the downswing, as was also pointed out by Dr David Williams in his book *The Science of the Golf Swing*. But if one analyses this curve (by Fourrier Analysis) it resolves into two simple sinusoidal curves (Fig. A2) in that:

a)   There is a main curve (G) whose half cycle time is equal to the downswing time. This I shall call the

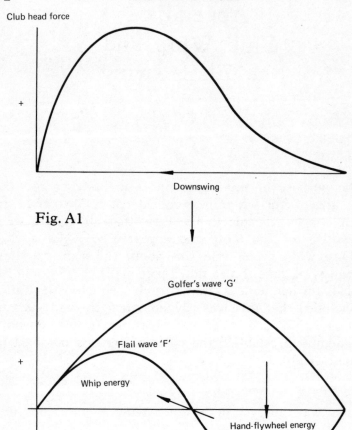

Club head force

+

Downswing

Fig. A1

Golfer's wave 'G'

Flail wave 'F'

Whip energy

+

Hand-flywheel energy

−

Fig. A2

Golfer's Wave since it also corresponds to the effort made by the golfer himself.

b)　There is a secondary wave (F) whose full cycle time is equal to the downswing time. This I shall call the *Flail Wave* and it has half the amplitude and twice the frequency of the Golfer's Wave. It is thus a 'second harmonic' of the Golfer's Wave. This wave relates to the club flail mechanics and has no net energy content since it has a balanced negative first half cycle followed by a positive half cycle.

The fact that the Flail Wave is at twice the frequency of the Golfer's Wave may well be related to the fact that in the downswing the club travels through about twice the angle of the arms. The club starts from behind the hands and arms but has to catch up with them at impact and typically the club will rotate through 260 degrees whilst the arms only rotate through 130 degrees. However, I do not make main use of this supporting point.

The chief enigma in the situation is to explain that first negative half cycle in the Flail Wave because it appears that energy must be 'vanishing' from the Golfer's Wave during the same phase. Equivalently, there is a sudden surge of energy from 'nowhere' in the second part of the downswing where the Flail Wave goes positive. Obviously the two facts are related to each other and the only explanation must be:

During the first half of the downswing about half the golfer's energy goes into storage and re-emerges in the second half of the downswing

But where is that energy stored? We know that its value is about 40 foot pounds. It goes into storage in the moving momentum of the hands and arms in the first half of the downswing. In this phase it is known that hand speed is about 35 feet per second and this would be associated with a weight of about two pounds to give an energy of 40 foot pounds. But this is just about the weight of the hands, wrists and a bit of the forearms and thus we account for the energy (the upper arms do not come into the matter appreciably since we are dealing with the energy in angular momentum which is prop-

ortional to the square of the velocities involved and thus
to the square of the radius about the shoulders).
   Thus:

> *The flail energy is first stored in the hands as*
> *kinetic ('flywheel') energy*

In the first part of the downswing about half the energy
goes into accelerating the club head whilst the other half
goes into flywheel storage in the hands zone. The
question which next arises is how does this energy
suddenly re-appear as extra club head energy in the
second part of the downswing. The explanation appears
to be (see Fig. A3):

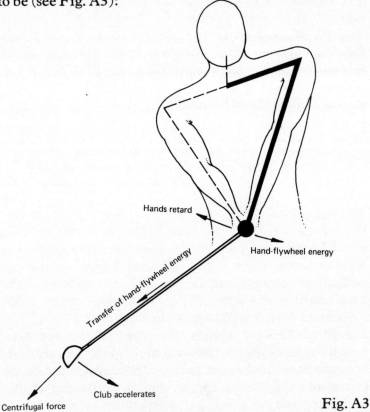

Fig. A3

a)   In the second part of the downswing the club head is developing considerable centrifugal forces of the order of 80 pounds and these are pulling along the length of the shaft.

b)   But during this phase there is a marked angle between the arms and the club shaft but the centrifugal force is irresistible to straighten out this angle by pulling on it.

c)   But this angle can only be straightened out if the club moves faster and *the hands move slower* and thus there is a transfer of the flywheel energy in the hands to the club head in accordance with the Laws of Conservation of Energy and Momentum. This energy transfer simply 'flows down the shaft'.

The short proof of this theory is the photographed fact that the hands do slow down towards impact to about half their former speed and thus transfer three-quarters of their flywheel energy to the club head ('three-quarters' because kinetic energy is proportional to the square of speed and at half speed the hands only retain one quarter of their former kinetic energy).

The two peaks in the downswing

This analysis leads to the thought that there are two peaks in the golf downswing:

1   The Golfer's Wave, the golfer's effort, peaks at half time of the downswing as shown at G of Fig. A2.

2   But the Flail Wave peaks at F of Fig. A2. and this is at three-quarters of downswing time. As far as the golfer is concerned he feels this effect as a backwards drag on the hands. This I shall call the Flail Drag and in resisting it the golfer adds speed to the

club head since he is providing more flywheel
energy in his hands to flow down the shaft.

Should the golfer power the flail drag?

In golf mythology there is a school of thought which
supports:

a) 'hitting late'
b) the importance of the hands and wrists in 'driving
through the ball'

My analysis might throw new light on this matter since
it has been shown elsewhere (*Flash* by Edgerton and
Killian) that the difference between a good golfer and a
poor golfer is that with the former the club head is
accelerating right up to impact. I suggest that this occurs
when the good golfer continues to power his 'hand
flywheel' through the second part of the downswing and
thus increase the energy available for club head acceleration through Flail Drag. Note that no hand or wrist
strength is required for this and all the golfer has to do is
keep his hands moving fast and the Flail Drag will extract
energy from this by its centrifugal pull (i.e. by trying to
straighten out the arm-club hinge).

Now it is well known that all the force exerted by the
golfer on the club is a pulling force but during the
downswing this pulling force changes direction relative
to the hands from pulling what is behind to pulling what
is in front of the golfer i.e. there is an angular change in
the pull direction relative to the hands.

But in the original pulling on the club at the start of
the downswing if there were no centrifugal effects, the
club head would only have the speed of the hands at, say,
35 feet a second, whereas in fact it accelerates to about
140 feet a second and multiplies its kinetic energy by a

factor of $(140/35)^2$ = sixteen times *by centrifugal effects alone*.

Now this leads to a conclusion which I had never realised before:

> *For practical purposes, the whole of the acceleration of the club head is due to centrifugal forces trying to straighten out the arm-shaft hinge*

But in order to maximise this effect it implies:

> *The power intent of the golfer should be to strive to keep his hands ahead of the club so that his 'hinge' enables the centrifugal forces to keep extracting energy from his hands*

Club whip and timing

Clearly a sense of timing comes into all this but the golfer does not feel the timing because all the forces are *pulling* on his hands while the golfer himself is trying to power his hand arc mainly *at right angles to the pull*. Thus although it would be highly desirable for the golfer to feel the timing of the Flail Wave *he cannot feel it in the direction of his hand arc* which is what matters to the golfer's psyche. But give the golfer a club whose whip timing is the same as the Flail Wave and he will feel the timing correctly because the club whip makes its presence felt along the hand arc. Thus I conclude:

> *If the golfer is to be assisted in his swing timing that assistance must be sensed in the same direction as his hand arc swing. But centrifugal forces from the club are all pulling across the*

hand arc and thus the golfer needs an instrument in his hands which supplies the correct timing in the direction of the hand arc. This assistance is provided by a club whose whip is of the same period as the flail wave.

Appendix 2
Psycho-Golf and
Sequential Word Drill

In this Appendix we consider the detailed technical nature whereby a sequence of skilled unit actions can be accurately programmed by a corresponding set of sequential single words. That such a development is achievable in practice is demonstrated by the use of this method on the barracks square. But in order to understand just how it all works and how it is learned requires a more complex analysis of the human psyche than that illustrated in Fig. 17.1.

The Skill Centre has two distinct functions as to 'Robotisms' and imagination

The lowest level of our Skill Centre consists of fixed conditioned reflexes or what I shall call 'Robotisms'. They are nervous complexes in that a given cause-trigger will produce a corresponding action-effect. Some typical examples are:

> Picking up the telephone when it rings
> Smiling at another person when he smiles at you

Robotisms are essentially 'trivial' since they call for no appreciable consciousness or adaptation.

But there is a quite distinct higher level of the Skill Centre which may be described as *imagination*. It combines both visual and sensing aspects as an inner world of imagination and it is this faculty which is responsible for our dreams, both daydreams and nightdreams. It is fundamentally an off-line faculty (as its dominance in dreams demonstrates) but it can also be on-line to our behaviour. When this is so it adds a dimension of drama and adaptability so that our behaviour becomes alive rather than robotic.

Typical examples of the on-line aspect of imagination are:

All forms of conscious assessment and anticipation ('foresight') related to physical events. The good tennis player relies on imagination to vary his shots to the disadvantage of his opponent, for example to 'catch him on the wrong foot'.

The combination of Robotisms and the imagination – the Skill-Tape

The two aspects of the Skill Centre can be combined into a single manifestation as:

$$Robotisms + Imagination = Skill\text{-}Tape$$

A Skill-Tape controls an act of behaviour by calling upon the conditioned reflex system for specifying the *details* of the behaviour while at the same time the imagination is constantly adapting its choice of such robotisms to suit its own purposes. In another book I am writing I show that the actions of a tennis player can be analysed into about 25 fundamental robotisms, i.e. possible unit detailed acts, but that the actual game of tennis has a far wider variety of possibilities due to the superimposition of imagination onto the situation which gives rise to highly adaptable Skill-Tapes. For example, let us imagine that one typical game in a tennis set calls for an average of 100 unit actions each of which is one of 25 varieties of robotism. But the permutations and combinations of the 25 robotisms in a chain of 100 acts each of which is selected by imagination leads to combinations of countless millions (25^{100} = 'trillions'). Thus it is the faculty of imagination which saves man from being a robot, since although each detail of his acts is robotic the chain of acts is non-robotic since it is permeated with the freedom provided by imagination.

It is for this dualistic reason that I call such behaviour a Skill-Tape with the term 'tape' implying robotic detail and the term 'skill' implying the modifying effect of imagination upon the system.

Ideas and words as triggers for the imagination

In any act of behaviour above the level of the trivial we are in the realm of imagination and Skill-Tapes. But we now have to take into account an even higher level of the human psyche and that is the verbal or word mind. Now I call the word mind 'higher' than the imagination because if used consciously a word can trigger a field of imagination into operation and this in turn will evoke a particular variety of Skill-Tapes. Of course words are not the only triggers for Skill-Tapes and if I suddenly feel thirsty then that physical fact can trigger the Skill-Tape for mixing myself a drink. Also our external senses can trigger Skill-Tapes into operation and if I see the traffic lights go red I shall put on the brakes to stop my car. Emotional states can also trigger Skill-Tapes and if I note that my wife is 'upset' then that will trigger a Skill-Tape in me to 'find what it is all about'. Broadly speaking, triggers for Skill-Tapes fall into two main groups:
1) Conscious verbal triggers which are under our conscious control

2)   Taciturn triggers which are more subconscious and
       may come from senses, instincts or emotions

In the context of Psycho-Golf I shall next limit myself to
the relationship between Conscious Verbal Triggers and
Skill-Tapes.

Psycho-Golf is triadic as to words, imagination and robotisms

It is clear that Psycho-Golf is psychologically triadic as
to the three components:

Golfing Formula Words	Triggers
Robotisms ⎫	
Imagination ⎭	Skill-Tapes

Thus if we wish to develop Psycho-Golf so that a given
Formula Word is effective in evoking a specific physical
posture or action then this involves two stages:

a)   The Formula Word must associate with our imagi-
       nation (mental picture) of what is implied to
       establish a Drill Word.

b)   In the light of the Drill Word, the imagination must
       practice the act or posture in collaboration with
       appropriate robotisms until a Skill-Tape is
       developed.

The final result is a Word-Triggered Skill-Tape. This
establishes the Psycho-Unit for Psycho-Golf.

Sequential Word-Triggered Skill-Tapes

Just as the soldier on the barracks square can learn a
number of acts or postures corresponding to such
command words as:

HALT SHUN STAND-EASY MARCH
RIGHT-WHEEL

. . . and so forth, so the Typical Golfer has to learn *three* such distinct Word-Triggered Skill-Tapes and apply them in sequential order so that they become integrated by the process of sequential addition as we considered in chapter 18. All this requires is that we remember the three-word Golfing Formula but at any time one need only recall one word and the termination of that stage will set us up to remember the following word and stage.

Index

185